# CAMBRIDGE TEXTS AND STUDIES IN THE HISTORY OF EDUCATION

*General Editors*

A. C. F. BEALES, A. V. JUDGES, J. P. C. ROACH

## ROBERT OWEN ON EDUCATION

# IN THIS SERIES

## Texts

*Fénelon on Education* edited by H. C. Barnard

*Friedrich Froebel* translated and edited
by Irene M. Lilley

*Matthew Arnold and the Education of the New Order*
edited by Peter Smith and Geoffrey Summerfield

*Robert Owen on Education* edited by Harold Silver

*James Mill on Education* edited by W. H. Burston

## Studies

*Education and the French Revolution*
by H. C. Barnard

OTHER TITLES IN PREPARATION

# ROBERT OWEN ON EDUCATION

SELECTIONS EDITED WITH AN
INTRODUCTION AND NOTES BY
HAROLD SILVER

CAMBRIDGE
AT THE UNIVERSITY PRESS
1969

Published by the Syndics of the Cambridge University Press
Bentley House, 200 Euston Road, London N.W.1
American Branch: 32 East 57th Street, New York, N.Y.10022

Library of Congress Catalogue Card Number: 69-10432
Standard Book Number: 521 07353 7

Printed in Great Britain
at the University Printing House, Cambridge
(Brooke Crutchley, University Printer)

# CONTENTS

# ACKNOWLEDGMENTS

I should like to acknowledge with gratitude the advice and help I have received from Professor A. V. Judges and the unfailing assistance given by Mr S. J. Teague and his staff at the library of Chelsea College of Science and Technology. I should also like to thank the Newcastle City Reference Library for copies of material from the Cowen papers in its possession, and the generous help of the library of the Co-operative Union, Manchester, in obtaining copies of correspondence in its collection of Owen papers.

H. S.

*Chelsea College of Science and Technology*

# INTRODUCTION

Robert Owen lived not so much a long life as a sequence of historical episodes. To follow him through the panorama of his activities is to follow at a fundamental level and at crucial points the complex history of the establishment of predominantly industrial, urban Britain. It is to touch some of the tenderest points of the suffering and bewilderment which accompanied it. It is to witness immense efforts to establish humane controls over the free-running processes of change, to build new hopes and objectives, to organise for their accomplishment. Cotton, factory legislation, education, trade unionism, cooperation, rationalism—each may have its heroes of a stature at least that of Owen, but in all of these, and more, Owen was there; never passively, always deeply involved in the attempt to cope sharply and seriously with the disconcerting implications of great changes. Owen was not a titan, but the episodes he fashioned add up to a contribution to British social development that was titanic.

He began, and in many respects remained, a child of the eighteenth century. He was born in 1771, at Newtown in Wales. He had a brief but probably effective small-town schooling, and educated himself beyond it. From the age of ten, first in Stamford, where he spent three years, then for a short time in London, and finally in Manchester, he worked as a draper's assistant. At the heart of the cotton revolution, in Manchester, he became involved in a partnership to produce cotton machinery and then, in 1792, he became manager of a large, modern cotton-spinning mill belonging to Peter

Drinkwater.[1] The following is Owen's summary of his Manchester career from this point:

I undertook to manage the spinning establishments of the Late Mr. Drinkwater of Manchester, at the latter place and at Northwich in Cheshire, in which occupation I remained three or four years. I then formed a partnership to carry on a cotton-spinning business with Messrs. Moulson and Scarth of Manchester; built the Chorlton Mills, and commenced a new firm, under the designation of the Chorlton Twist Company, along with Messrs. Borrodale and Atkinson, of London, and Messrs. H. and J. Barton and Co. of Manchester.[2]

In the 1790s, in Manchester, he learned and improved upon the techniques of fine spinning. He was also schooled in industrial administration, and—among the intellectual circles of the town—in the language of the eighteenth-century Enlightenment. This was the first episode.

The second began when in 1800, as a partner in the Chorlton Twist Co., he took over management of the New Lanark Cotton Mills, which he had persuaded his partners to buy. Through several changes of partners, resistance from the population of the village and elsewhere, he pursued for a quarter of a century his schemes to establish a new pattern of industrial life, a new approach to the social problems of early nineteenth-century Britain. He improved housing and food supplies, the appearance and health of the village. He reorganised the

---

[1] Accounts of Owen's early life rely on *The Life of Robert Owen by himself* (1857). An important corrective is W. H. Chaloner, *Robert Owen, Peter Drinkwater and the Early Factory System in Manchester* (1954).

[2] Written in 1817, reprinted in *The Life of Robert Owen*, IA (supplementary appendix, 1858), 82.

mills and won the confidence of the workers. He proclaimed a public gospel of tolerance and kindness and worked to accomplish them. He dispensed with the employment of pauper apprentices, raised the age at which children were admitted to employment, and created the first system of infant education in Britain. Against a background of the reluctant or tentative provision of education in England, and the declining standard of parish education in Scotland, he built a model for children up to the age of ten which no one in the nineteenth century was able to surpass.

His reputation was by the mid 1810s internationally established. *A New View of Society*, which he wrote in 1812–13, and first sold publicly in 1816, is one of the crucial texts of British social history and his contemporaries discussed it as such. He had a message of social reorganisation which he began to preach more and more emphatically, and he accepted the challenge in 1824 to create a model community in the United States.

At the beginning of this, the third episode, Owen had long been an associate of the great and the powerful. To list those with whom he corresponded, mixed, discussed and argued would be to list most of the names of importance in Britain in the first quarter of the nineteenth century. When he bought from the Rappite Community their land at Harmony, Indiana, he hoped to demonstrate by an experiment in community organisation what could be the basis for a whole international regeneration. His major attention, though not the whole of his time, between 1824 and 1829, was concentrated on the American New Harmony project, but slowly and relentlessly it failed. By the end of the twenties Owen had lost a great deal of his fortune, and most of his

I-2

influential friends. Owen the successful cotton employer and social theorist had, in the difficult years at the end of the Napoleonic wars, been of interest to them. Owen the social experimentalist and propagandist, when the great and the powerful had regained their composure and confidence, was not.

In the face of disaster or defeat of any kind Owen never faltered. When, after 1829, he began to pick up the threads, he found to his surprise that a new audience and new allies had emerged in Britain. The fourth episode lasted until 1834, and in it Owen became one of the most important pioneers of the British labour movement. Owen's pioneering had, indeed, begun long before, but only as a by-product of his proclamation of a creed of community and humanity. Paternalist then and always, he had seen no further in *A New View of Society*, for example, than a vision of a humane, paternalistic reformation of society. Now he found working men who accepted his vision, but wished to take part in implementing it. Working-class radicals, after difficult years of repression, alert in the twenties to new means of organisation and receptive to ideals which offered any prospect of challenging, changing or by-passing the relentless march of an inhumane society, saw a message of hope in the doctrines of Owen. Onto other traditions, other ideals, they grafted Owen's vision of community, of education, of a society founded on principles of cooperation.

For five years or so, hesitantly at first, Owen became absorbed in the activities of a politically and organisa-tionally reawakening labour movement; he had dis-covered a force which derived at least some of its vigour from his ideas; he sought to harness it (and it was not unwilling to be harnessed) to attain a tangible vision.

Working-class and radical cooperators had been trying to establish Owenite communities since the very beginning of the 1820s. The first such attempt was the London Co-operative and Economical Society, established in 1821; its progress was recorded in *The Economist*, begun in the same year to explain, it announced, 'the new system of Society projected by Robert Owen'. Orbiston, the first major Owenite experiment in community organisation, began in 1825. By the time of Owen's return from the New World, the number of Owenite cooperative societies ran into hundreds.

This was part of the ground out of which Owen's fourth episode arose. It witnessed, under the driving impetus of Owen himself and the growing register of Owenite thinkers and organisers, the brief period of Owen's mass working-class basis and influence. From 1831 dates the national efflorescence of the movement under Owen's leadership, aimed at cooperative effort towards the establishment of communities. From 1832 date Owen's attempts to establish the Labour Exchange as a means of interchanging cooperatively produced goods through the medium of 'labour notes' which reflected the value of the producer's labour. From 1832 date Owen's first newspaper, *The Crisis*, and his first organisation aimed at popular propaganda—the Association of the Intelligent and Well Disposed of the Industrious Classes for removing the Causes of Ignorance and Poverty by Education and Employment. From 1832 also date the beginnings of the commitment of wide sections of the trade union movement to the Owenite cause, culminating in his Grand National Consolidated Trades Union with its dramatic but short-lived existence in 1834.

By 1835 Owen, now well into his sixties, was plunging into his fifth period. He had lost his mass organisational support. If he had been over-eager, and too much caught up in the passions of class warfare, his socialism (as it now was) and his free-thought crusade were matters for rational, reasonable persuasion. From the mid thirties Owen's organisation frequently changed its name and the title of its newspaper (though for most of the time *The New Moral World* was the principal part), but its central purpose was, by careful organisation, reasoned debate and constant propaganda, to win over the minds of men.

Owen died on 17 November 1858. For the quarter of a century since Owenite trade unionism and cooperation had reached their zenith and declined, he and his organised followers had patiently reiterated their message of human community. But the dynamic of social movements, having absorbed Owenite energies, had by then come to lie elsewhere.

This brief narrative, of course, does less than justice even to the outline of Owen's life, which is, in most respects, a familiar story. To some aspects of the narrative we shall return; others, Owen's writings in the selection here made, including from his *Life*, will illuminate. There are, however, three precise questions to which we need to devote attention. First, if a preoccupation with education was a constant through all Owen's episodes, how did he arrive at it? Secondly, what, particularly in the eyes of his contemporaries, were the salient points of attraction in his educational ideas? And, thirdly, what happened to them?

'It must have been desperately hard', H. L. Beales has reflected, 'to know what was going on in the earlier phase of industrialization.'[1] It was hard because the growth of industry, its new disciplines and demands brought confusion. Its impact on the patterns of lives in new urban concentrations brought confusion. Its effect on traditional skills, its disturbance of traditional family and social routines and expectations, brought confusion. Although industrialisation did not effect a total cataclysm, the final decades of the eighteenth century and the early ones of the nineteenth did experience great discontinuities of social change. In the first half century or so of major industrialisation, however, the new productive developments wrestled with resilient traditions. Much that we have associated with nineteenth-century developments was, in fact, as Peter Laslett has suggested in *The World we have lost* (1965), a feature of pre-industrial society. Much of pre-industrial England, conversely, persisted longer than we have sometimes allowed for. Survivals, as G. Kitson Clark puts it,

are in fact to be found round every Victorian corner. Habits, patterns of behaviour, attitudes of mind, conditions of living which had come down from the eighteenth century persisted not only in the life and practices of the aristocracy but also in the ways of life and thought, and where there was not much conscious thought in the instincts and customs, of people much lower down the social scale.[2]

The industrial revolution clearly did not create the poverty, or the disease, malnutrition and low expectation of life that were outstanding aspects of the new towns: it intensified them.

It was in the cotton industry, and in Lancashire above

---

[1] *The Industrial Revolution 1750–1850* (1958 ed.), p. 20.
[2] *The Making of Victorian England* (1962), p. 59.

all, that the tensions of the new industrialism were at their most acute. A great deal of discussion has taken place about the complex factors which firmly projected Britain in the last two decades of the eighteenth century into a self-sustaining industrial revolution. The central fact, however, is clear: some time in the 1780s 'the shackles were taken off the productive power of human societies, which henceforth became capable of the constant, rapid and up to the present limitless multiplication of men, goods and services'.[1] Developments in agriculture, trade, technology, transport and the minds of men had combined, by the time Owen entered the cotton industry, to establish a new industrial order clustered around cotton. For the first time in history 'a great staple industry had been established on the basis of a natural resource that could not be domestically produced'.[2] Owen had, in coming to Manchester, come to the hub of these developments and of rapid, uncontrolled urban growth.

'Until the reign of George III', it has been suggested, 'a town was regarded as improving a landscape. A city was a glorious and beautiful thing, an object to be proud of.'[3] The industrial town, however, in its early stages was not *regarded* as anything; it was not intended as anything, it simply grew, and with it grew the human problems which are familiar landmarks of nineteenth-century social history, including the loss of an understood framework of social relationships and behaviour that had been characteristic of the lives of people before they crowded into towns.

It is important, however, to keep sight of the fact

[1] E. J. Hobsbawm, *The Age of Revolution* (1962), p. 28.
[2] Phyllis Deane, *The First Industrial Revolution* (1965), p. 64.
[3] William Ralph Inge, *The Victorian Age* (1922), p. 20.

that many features of social life were continuous across the reaches of the industrial revolution. The beautiful town had also been a repository of disease; the haphazardly growing town offered a more concentrated picture of negligent and mortal social organisation. In describing the gamut of loss, adjustment and pain through which industrialisation caused many sections of the people to pass, Edward Thompson reminds us of both 'the continuing traditions and the context that has changed'. We must not, in emphasising the newness of the cotton mills, underestimate 'the continuity of political and cultural traditions in the making of working-class communities'.[1]

Even the difficult and important debate that has taken place about the effect of the industrial revolution on the standard of living in the half century or more from 1780 has been concerned with—overall—small shifts in averages: 'whichever way it went, the net change was relatively slight'.[2]

Manchester, however, and its population, were not averages. Nor, indeed, can the industrial revolution as a whole be thought of very profitably in terms of averages: 'The older "cataclysmic" view of the Industrial Revolution must still be accepted...The process of industrialisation is necessarily painful. It must involve the erosion of traditional patterns of life. But it was carried through with exceptional violence in Britain.'[3] Manchester has, of course, a long history. The cotton trade had become important in the late seventeenth century, and by 1729 the town had a population of about 15,000. It had even petitioned for the creation of a

---

[1] E. P. Thompson, *The Making of the English Working Class* (1963), pp. 24 and 193.
[2] Deane, *The First Industrial Revolution*, p. 250.
[3] Thompson, *The Making of the English Working Class*, p. 445.

university in Manchester in 1640.[1] Its population was over 40,000 in the late 1780s, was over 70,000 by 1801, and reached 142,000 by 1831. Manchester and Salford together had 90,400 in 1800. Fifty years later they had 388,500.[2] In the short and the long run this growth and all that it involved were of the order of a cataclysm. By the thirties and forties Manchester had become the symbol of industrial civilisation. It had also become the symbol of urban disaster. It was a totally new kind of urban phenomenon, and to a Robert Owen, out of Newtown and Stamford, it must, in the 1790s even, have been of cataclysmic proportions. It is from this starting-point of his involvement in the process of industrialisation and urbanisation that Owen set out towards a New View of Society.

If it was hard, in this period, to know 'what was going on', it was the finding of bearings that was hardest. Owen found an intellectual position, a tradition and a momentum of conviction in the Enlightenment. It is necessary, if we are to arrive at a rounded answer to the first of the questions we are seeking to answer—how Owen arrived at his preoccupation with education—to understand what he made of his antecedents. In the history of English thought this is a relationship of no small importance.

The facts we have of *how* Owen arrived at his intellectual stance are brief and here only of passing interest. In Manchester in the nineties he was a member of the extremely important Literary and Philosophical Society and was close to its President, Dr Thomas

[1] Michael Sadler, 'The story of education in Manchester', in W. H. Brindley (ed.), *The Soul of Manchester* (1929).
[2] Asa Briggs, *Victorian Cities* (1963), p. 85; Adna Ferrin Weber, *The Growth of Cities* (1963 ed.), p. 450.

Percival, a learned and distinguished figure in the circles of the eighteenth-century European Enlightenment. Owen had, if his autobiography is to be believed, acquired through his early reading a scepticism about religion; and among men such as this, and in the climate of opinion of the early nineties, he learned the syntax of eighteenth-century rationalism. The accents in which he spoke for the remainder of his life were those he learned, directly or indirectly, from Helvétius and to a lesser extent from Rousseau, Godwin and Mary Wollstonecraft.

The crucial feature of Owen's rationalism was that he was without history, and rationalism itself is an unhistorical mode of thought. For Owen, as for the eighteenth-century French thinkers, the key to all social problems lay in the nature of social institutions. If they were degenerate, it was in the supremacy of reason that the lever for their reformation was to be found. It was a philosophy of reason, and of change: 'The advantage of man was their principle, and the value of speculation was judged by its definite service to humanity...The problem for the human race being to reach a state of felicity by its own powers, these thinkers believed that it was soluble by the gradual triumph of reason over prejudice and knowledge over ignorance.'[1] The important fact, Carl Becker has pointed out, is that eighteenth-century philosophers 'did not ask how society had come to be what it was, but how it could be made better than it was'.[2]

We have only in recent decades begun to examine clearly, through eyes other than those of the nineteenth

[1] J. B. Bury, *The Idea of Progress* (1955 ed.), pp. 161–2.
[2] *The Heavenly City of the Eighteenth-Century Philosophers* (1932), p. 97.

century, the precise nature and accomplishments of eighteenth-century thought and culture.

In its original outlines, [Stuart Hughes has commented] the philosophy of the Enlightenment appears far less intellectualistic than as usually characterized, and its presumed fondness for mechanistic and materialistic explanations and naive faith in human progress stand revealed as largely the product of subsequent critical distortion.

Hughes stresses the

open, undogmatic quality of most eighteenth-century thought, its flexible use of the concept of reason, and its sympathetic understanding for 'sensibility' and 'the passions'... Certain ethical postulates characteristic of the eighteenth century—chief among them the insistence, *where possible*, on rational solutions and humane behavior—represent an abiding legacy of overriding importance.[1]

The insistence on rational solutions and the judgment of the value of speculation by 'its definite service to humanity' were the sources from which, with their different emphases, sprang both the utilitarianism of Jeremy Bentham and Tom Paine and the political radicalism of the 1790s. Rationalism and utilitarianism had an eighteenth-century English history, but it was through the impact of the French Enlightenment, on William Godwin in particular, that the tradition reached Owen, and it was in Godwin and Owen, not in utilitarian philosophy and its works, that the conjoint legacy of 'rational solutions and humane behavior' reasserted itself in an industrial environment.

The line of descent of the rational, humane and unhistorical framework of Owen's thought is from Claude Adrien Helvétius. Helvétius was a figure of considerable

[1] H. Stuart Hughes, *Consciousness and Society* (1959), pp. 27–8.

importance in the circles of the eighteenth-century French *philosophes*, and one of the most consistently radical. His *De l'esprit*, published in 1758, went beyond the work of his contemporaries in the systematised form of its attack on church and state, and its total environmental philosophy. Even many of his fellow philosophers were 'frightened at seeing the full implications of their own theories' and hurt by his 'denial of individual, class, and national superiorities'.[1] Helvétius died in the year of Owen's birth, and *De l'homme* was published posthumously. In it he elaborates more fully his psychological and educational principles. He identifies himself with Locke and the doctrine of sensation: 'All the operations of the mind are reducible to sensation.'[2] There are no such things as innate ideas; and 'no individual is born good or bad'.[3]

Section v of the book is devoted to disputing some of the premises and confusions he finds in Rousseau, who in *Emile* was prepared to accept that such sentiments as virtue and justice are 'innate in the heart of man'. Helvétius asserts emphatically that 'Man, born without ideas or character, and indifferent to good and evil, has no gift from nature but corporeal sensibility; that in his cradle he is nothing; that his virtues and vices, his factitious passions, his talents, his prejudices, and even his self-love, are all acquired.'[4] The majority of the book is devoted to demonstrating his thesis that education is all-powerful. Education is for him, in fact, everything that impinges on the sensations; for two people to be exactly alike 'they should be in precisely the same positions and the same circumstances. Now such an

[1] Mordecai Grossman, *The Philosophy of Helvétius* (1926), p. 17.
[2] Helvétius, *A Treatise on Man*, trans. W. Hooper (1810), I, 96.
[3] *Ibid.* II, 11.          [4] *Ibid.* II, 24.

hypothesis is impossible: it is therefore evident, that no two persons can receive the same instructions...it is impossible for two men to acquire precisely the same ideas.'[1] He offers examples of the dependence of character, individual, tribal and national, on external circumstances and induction through training. Rousseau had adduced notions of man's natural goodness; Helvétius does not deny the existence of good men, 'but the humanity of these is the effect of their education, not their nature. Had these men been born among the Iroquois, they would have adopted their barbarous customs.'[2] The hunting skills of the Indian, the knowledge of the civilised man, the arrogance of the priest, for example, demonstrate the dependence of character on environment and training. 'Education makes us what we are.'[3]

It is difficult to over-emphasise the importance of the clarity and uncompromising nature of Helvétius' work, with its stress on the total influence of external circumstances, and its insistence on rational government and educational provision. It was not an original exercise in the heyday of the French Enlightenment to attack the constricting effects of corrupt institutions, and to argue that man, 'born free', is in the chains of a degenerate social environment. What was original, and earned persecution, was reaching out for the full implications of these doctrines, the adjustment of a theory of self-interest, one of the products of social training, to a rational view of social organisation. Not only could self-interest be made to coincide with public interest, but progress, through knowledge, 'is a force in the creating of a better society and a better individual...darkness and despotism are impediments in the path of human

---

[1] Helvétius, I, 12–13.     [2] *Ibid.* II, 23.     [3] *Ibid.* II, 405.

progress'.[1] It was a total theme more consistently revolutionary in its implications than that of Rousseau, more consistently rationalist than even that of Voltaire.

The ideas of Helvétius became quickly accessible in England, and he visited the country in 1764. William Godwin's *Enquiry concerning Political Justice*, first published in 1793, relies heavily on the kind of ideas Helvétius had elaborated and made part of the heritage that was eagerly sought for by radical British thinkers in the 1790s. We cannot follow Godwin, as we could not follow Helvétius, in any detail, but it will be useful briefly to trace the language of Helvétius in its English setting. 'The actions and dispositions of mankind', Godwin sets out to demonstrate, 'are the offspring of circumstances and events, and not of any original determination that they bring into the world.' Such actions and dispositions 'flow entirely from the operation of circumstances and events acting upon a faculty of receiving sensible impressions'. Godwin dismisses 'innate principles of judgment' and, like Helvétius, seeks to demonstrate that character is interchangeable with circumstances. 'There is for the most part no essential difference', he affirms, 'between the child of the lord and of the porter...the child of the lord, if changed in the cradle, would scarcely find any greater difficulty than the other, in learning the trade of his foster father.' Unlike Helvétius, Godwin partly accepts 'the real differences that exist between children at the period of their birth', but like Helvétius stresses that 'education never can be equal. The inequality of external circumstances in two beings whose situations

---

[1] Grossman, *The Philosophy of Helvétius*, p. 21.
[2] *Enquiry concerning Political Justice*, edited by F. E. L. Priestley (1946), I, 26–7.

most nearly resemble, is so great as to baffle all power of calculation.'[1] Like Helvétius he proceeds from such assumptions to 'a general delineation of the principles of rational society'.[2]

It will be evident from the texts below how close Owen's formulations are to these two writers. We are here not concerned with formal derivations but with the operation in the writings and work of Owen of a tradition. There may well have been other influences, but there can be no doubt that the rationalist tradition here suggested was the dominant one even in the earliest formulations Owen made of his doctrines. At a public dinner in Glasgow in 1812, in honour of Joseph Lancaster, Owen presided, and heralded the doctrine of circumstances he was to elaborate more fully in *A New View of Society* in that and the following year. What, he asked at the dinner, causes bodily and mental differences that exist among men? 'They are wholly and solely', he answered, 'the effects of that education which I have described. Man becomes a wild ferocious savage, a cannibal, or a highly civilised and benevolent being, according to the circumstances in which he may be placed from his birth.' Owen, like Helvétius, used the terms 'education' and 'circumstances' interchangeably; and the doctrine embodied in these two sentences is, then, that of the degeneracy of social institutions. He goes on to ask 'whether we have any influence over these circumstances; if we can command any of them; and if we can, to what extent'.[3] Owen, like his predecessors, was concerned with change. If man is everywhere in chains, if social institutions are, as the eighteenth-century philosophers considered, 'obviously contrary

[1] *Enquiry*, pp. 37–9.  [2] *Ibid.* p. 183.
[3] *Life*, appendix A, 249.

to the essential nature of man, obviously needing to be set right', then rational and humane solutions need to be applied—'and that speedily'.[1]

It is, under these lights, easier to see how Owen came by an all-embracing theory. Sensitive to human as well as industrial changes, he was aware both of the standards and traditions that stretched back into the recent pre-industrial past and of the struggles taking place in men's minds and lives to preserve, to adapt, to prevent. He found his theory, therefore, in a world in which ideas and schemes and ideals played a part in men's lives as they had not done since the middle of the seventeenth century. The 1790s did not inaugurate radical speculation and radical political thought in Britain. 'If', it has been rightly said, 'the French Revolution caused Britain to vibrate, it was because the nation was already tensely strung.'[2] But the 1790s were, for all that, the beginning of new kinds of struggles to find solutions to social and political problems, and to organise action to achieve them. The French Revolution was in serious respects, as Carlyle understood, an English one too: '...not a French revolt only; no, a European one; full of stern monition to all countries of Europe. These Chartisms, Radicalisms, Reform Bill, Tithe Bill, and infinite other discrepancy, and acrid argument and jargon that there is yet to be, are *our* French Revolution.'[3] The industrial, urban developments, with their greater mobilities, uncertainties and angers, were, in Britain, part of the complex of new gropings towards political reform and greater civic and social freedoms. This was

[1] Becker, *The Heavenly City*, p. 98.
[2] L. G. Johnson, *The Social Evolution of Industrial Britain* (1963), p. 9.
[3] *Chartism* (1888 ed.), p. 27.

the atmosphere in which Owen, in his twenties, found in Manchester's industrial and intellectual life the ideas by which he could—he was convinced—set things right, and that speedily!

Owen moved to New Lanark at the beginning of the century, and it is against the backcloth of his activities there that we have to see the period of his formulation of a philosophy, ideals and policies. He had adopted a philosophy of reason, and he expected, like those from whom he learned his doctrine, that through the rational exposition of rational solutions, reason would inevitably prevail. In the quarter century at New Lanark, Owen bestrides the reasonableness of the Enlightenment and the nineteenth-century preoccupation with social action —not political action, because, wherever Owen's doctrines led him, it was never into anything that one could properly call action for political reform. Although he was involved in popular movements, he was of the eighteenth century; he was the philosopher grappling with the rational reordering of the bases of society, not with what he considered to be the superficialities of political agitation. He had been left unmoved by political radicalism in Manchester in the early nineties.

We have seen, in partial answer to our question about the derivation of Owen's ideas, how he arrived at a philosophy. What this meant more specifically in terms of ideas about education will emerge from the discussion of our second question—what to his contemporaries was attractive about his ideas. The central point in both connections is that Owen not only adopted and elaborated a philosophy, he saw its vindication stand out more and more clearly in the practice of New Lanark. 'Always,' Raymond Williams has commented, 'it is

Owen's experience that is impressive—the lived quality of his new view of society.'[1] It is this combination of a consistent view of society and a 'lived quality' of experience and sympathy that separates Owen off from the majority of early nineteenth-century utilitarians on the one hand and philanthropists on the other. Owen was incapable of pursuing a policy which, like Chadwick's Poor Law reform of the 1830s, was social engineering through a deliberate programme of harsh deterrence. Although Owen's views derived ultimately from the same sources as those of James Mill or Francis Place, and though he occasionally borrowed aspects of their economic doctrines, he had too deep and understanding a sympathy with the victims of industrialism to accept the strait-jacket of the utilitarian programme. Paternalist and politically conservative though he was, he was also in no sense a charitable philanthropist.

The early days of growing urban disaster saw, indeed, charitable efforts of an extensive and distinguished kind. Men like Peter Bedford, a contemporary of Owen's, active in the relief of destitution among the Spitalfields silk-loom weavers and the investigation of the causes of juvenile delinquency, and known widely among the criminals of London, whom he tried to befriend and rescue—men like this (and William Allen, one of Owen's partners at New Lanark, was a friend of Bedford's) were in a tradition and enhanced it. Their Christianity and their ethic, however, were instruments of rescue and retrieval. Their form of 'lived experience' and sympathy was a different thing from a new view of society.[2] Spoken or unspoken, the charitable

---

[1] *Culture and Society 1780–1950* (1961 Penguin ed.), p. 46.
[2] See William Tallick, *Peter Bedford, the Spitalfields Philanthropist* (1865); Allen, *Life of William Allen* (1846).

impulse was part of a doctrine of moral and financial responsibility:

The philanthropist...knows that the distinctions in civil society are the result of principles orginally planted in man ...But he asks, whether it can be supposed that so great a disparity in outward circumstances was designed by Providence chiefly for the sake of the few; or not rather that, by the accumulation of capital, intellectual as well as material, the means of happiness and virtue might be disseminated throughout the mass.[1]

Such views were not necessarily the mainspring of all charitable attempts to cope with inequalities in the early nineteenth century, and this would not serve as a suitable text for a discussion of the activities of an Elizabeth Fry, for example. The doctrine of the responsibility of the favoured towards the unfavoured is, however, implied in philanthropic activity. Owen did, indeed, visit Newgate prison with Mrs Fry, and his advocacy of community principles in the Press in 1817 included a commendation of her work. The female prisoners had passed from a state of 'filth, bad habits, vice, crime—from the depth of degradation and wretchedness—to cleanliness, good habits, and comparative comfort and cheerfulness' under Mrs Fry's influence over a period of three months. Her activities, he pointed out, confirmed his own experience.[2] He was impressed, but he had already at New Lanark been engaged on schemes which, however close their humanitarian principles might be to those of the philanthropic rescue-workers, were designed to prevent, not just to

[1] Anon., *Essays on the Principles of Charitable Institutions* (1836), pp. 117–19.
[2] *Life,* IA, 78–9.

alleviate. He was, he realised, already working on a grander scale.

Owen, even when accepting that 'disparity in outward circumstances' was part of the natural order of things, was not concerned with a moral approach to the relief of distress. He was concerned with the causes of distress. Like the philanthropist he was concerned with the fate of individuals; but unlike the philanthropist he was concerned to remould society on their behalf. Owen did not argue from position or wealth; he argued from reason. He was not, of course, the only person in early nineteenth-century Britain who combined new views with intensive experience and activity. From the turmoil of the 1790s onwards, the historian of ideas, of social and political movements, has many major figures to consider. There were those who, like Richard Carlile, followed the lead of Tom Paine, and combined new views on religion with, for example, action for freedom of the Press. There were, more decorously, James Mill, Henry Brougham, Harriet Martineau, to name only a few, who combined utilitarian political economy with activity to diffuse 'useful knowledge' and reform social institutions of various kinds. There was William Cobbett, whose views were probably neither newer nor older than Robert Owen's but who strode through some of the decades of the early nineteenth century as a veritable redeemer. The precise qualities of Owen that mark him off from other reformers will appear below in the evidence of his writings. The one central factor, and the one that brings us closer to the questions we have asked about Owen, is the centrality to his doctrines of salient and characteristic views about education. *A New View of Society* is about political economy, about the organisation of social life, about Owen's particular experience at New Lanark, but it is above all about education, and is one of the master texts of British educational history. Other figures already mentioned, notably Brougham, featured prominently in the educational debates and labours of the early nineteenth century. None, however, brought to education the same energy and imagination. For none was it so broad in conception. None approached it with the same sense of dedication, and even awe.

For Owen, as we have seen, education and circumstances were inextricably linked. They are the core of all his formulations of opinion and policy from his first public statements of the early 1810s, and it is always with this sense of respect and drama that he approaches them. In his *Report to the County of Lanark* (1820), for example, he has been asked to set out his proposals to remedy the evil of a 'general want of employment, at wages sufficient to support the family of a working man beneficially to the community'. His remedies are embedded in a wide-ranging survey of problems of political economy and currency, spade cultivation and industrial progress. The overall remedy, one which Owen has been advocating for three or four years by this time, is the establishment of the poor in agricultural village-communities. He outlines in some detail the various proposed arrangements for cultivation, feeding, lodging and clothing the population. Then, three-quarters through the Report comes the announcement which makes everything that preceded it seem like mere preliminaries:

Your Reporter has now to enter upon the most interesting portion of this division of the subject, and, he may add, the most important part of the economy of human life, with reference to the science of the influence of circumstances over the well-being and happiness of mankind, and to the full power and control which men may now acquire over those circumstances.

He goes on to explain his doctrine of character formation. Knowledge, he begins (in terms which relate back to Locke, Hartley, Helvétius and Godwin), is acquired 'through the evidence of our senses'. This being the case, it is clear that infants are from birth 'continually subject to impressions derived from the circumstances around them; which impressions, combined with their natural qualities ... do truly determine the character of the individual through every period of life'.[1] In drawing out the implications of this theory for the provision of education Owen is, in fact, enunciating not a *part* of his doctrine, but the *whole* of it in microcosm. His theory of education is the open road to a new world. This total commitment to a view of society in which education is not a stage but a constant dynamic is the real heartbeat of Owen, and nowhere is the totality of the commitment more visible than in *A New View of Society* and the *Report to the County of Lanark*. Whether he be discussing crime and punishment, employment and unemployment, production and distribution, religion and tolerance, he makes us constantly aware that education is, in fact, 'the most important part of the economy of human life'.

His commitment is not, one must re-emphasise, a purely theoretical one. His *New View* is not of an abstract society, but of one in which New Lanark (as well as Newgate) exists to provide the demonstration and the certainty. By the time he published *A New View of Society* Owen had achieved a great deal in the village, and had extensive plans for the development of his

[1] See below, pp. 181-2.

23

educational work—achievements and plans which are outlined in *A New View* itself. Only under his third partnership (which included William Allen and Jeremy Bentham) was Owen able to implement these plans fully, and open (in January 1816) his renowned Institution for the Formation of Character, including the infant schools. This was, for Owen, no ordinary occurrence. 'From this day', he announced to the inhabitants of New Lanark at the opening, 'a change must take place; a new era must commence; the human intellect, through the whole extent of the earth, hitherto enveloped by the grossest ignorance and superstition, must begin to be released from its state of darkness.'[1] This brings us to the edge of a difficult aspect of what have been described as 'the several projects that took shape in Owen's noble and discursive reveries'[2] from about 1816—the close reference to experience alongside what becomes not so much a New View as a New Vision.

Owen had negotiated the purchase of New Lanark from David Dale (whose daughter he subsequently married) on behalf of the Chorlton Twist Co. Dale had been, as Owen was ready to admit, an employer of relatively benevolent views; Owen had begun, however, to reshape New Lanark on the basis not of benevolence but of a philosophy of living. By the time he opened his institution Owen had successfully overcome a great deal of resistance and difficulty. He had had—as a Manchester cotton-merchant—slowly to win the confidence of a hostile Scottish populace, and their support for his attacks on dirt, disease, drunkenness and theft. He had had to overcome resistance to his plans from his

[1] In *A New View of Society and other Writings* (1949 Everyman ed.), p. 97.
[2] J. L. and B. Hammond, *The Rise of Modern Industry* (1966 ed.), p. 260.

first two sets of partners, alarmed above all at the generosity of his educational schemes; he had had to prevent them from buying him out of the mills, and to find a third and final set of sympathetic partners. He had been successful on all counts. The names of Owen and New Lanark were by now widely known. His new partnership itself reflected the standing he had achieved. The partners were all men of eminence in commercial and public life. One, Bentham, was a dominant figure in the European intellectual world. Others had distinguished records of activity in public causes, including the support of Lancaster's educational plans. William Allen, prominent member of the Society of Friends, active in many movements, was treasurer of the British and Foreign School Society and during this period was 'looked upon by the Whigs as the national spokesman for Dissent on matters of education'.[1]

Owen's opinions were being sought and listened to, in a period of difficult economic conditions, uncertainty and confusion, when his conviction and determined tone were widely attractive. He was convinced that he had discovered *the* answer to society's problems. If New Lanark could work, why could the rest of the world not operate on like principles? This was the source both of his schemes for communities and of his visionary tone of voice. There was unemployment and distress. Could the country not at least solve this simple problem? His answer, in the London newspapers, in 1817, was that, in fact,

the country possesses the most ample means to attain this object... Those means consist of land unemployed; land

[1] R. G. Cowherd, *The Politics of English Dissent* (1959), p. 19. For a brief account of Allen see David Salmon, *William Allen*, reprinted from the *Educational Record* (1905).

imperfectly cultivated; money employed unprofitably; manual powers of labour idle, demoralising, and consequently generating every kind of evil in society; artificial or mechanical agency almost unlimited, and which might be made available for the most important purposes. These are the means which, if properly combined and put into action, would soon relieve the country from poverty and its attendant evils.

How was this to be done?

By bringing them all into useful and profitable combinations, so as to create limited communities of individuals, on the principle of united labour and expenditure, having their basis in agriculture, and in which all should have mutual and common interests.[1]

By 1817, then, Owen had behind him considerable experience of industry, and an awareness of its productive potential. He had experience of human responsiveness to improved conditions. He had experience of overcoming difficulties and opposition. He had a philosophy which, he was now sure, worked.

It is not surprising, therefore, that one of the elements in his 'reveries' came to be a conviction of the imminence of the millennium. Owen, it is perhaps important to point out, was not alone in his pursuit of a vision. A vision of a new society was an ingredient, from the enthusiasms of the early 1790s to those of the Chartists, in the writings of the radicals and reformers, the hopeful and the confused and the distressed, Cobbett and Richard Carlile, Feargus O'Connor and Bronterre O'Brien, the religious millenarians and the phrenologists. Owen was simply one of the most consistent, and most unhistorical. He was from this period on to see the

[1] *Life*, 1A, 69.

world perpetually on the brink of momentous trans-
formation. There are glimpses of this theme in *A New
View*. They occur frequently in his letters and addresses
of 1817. In 1818 he addressed a memorial to the governments of Europe and America, telling them that 'the
dominion of Ignorance, of Fraud, and of Violence, is
also on the point of terminating'.[1] The word 'millennium' itself in the 1830s became a constant part of his
vocabulary, and in 1835 part of the title of his newspaper. In the 1810s and 1820s, however, this visionary
element in Owen did not diminish his stature. His
public attacks on religion from 1817, at a time when
government was committed to repressive legislation and
action, did weaken his influence among the powerful.
Owen's place in the public imagination as pilot of an
advance to better, more humane social conditions was
by this time, however, secure.

We have traced the route Owen took to a conviction of
the power of education, and the extracts below are
concerned for the most part with his statement of the
total system within which this conviction was a driving
force, and with the system of education at New Lanark.
On the latter it is at this point barely necessary to com-
ment. He began by being sympathetic towards the
labours of Lancaster in particular to establish the
monitorial system. Limited and inefficient though it
was, this movement must be seen against the lingering
opposition to education of any kind for the poor. A
pamphlet published in 1822 by the Rev. J. Twist on
*The Policy of Educating the Poor* argued that current
schemes of 'refining the intellectual powers of the
lower classes, were it practicable, would put the whole

[1] *Life*, IA, 211.

community into an unnatural state of excitement'. Encouragement for the lower classes to entertain 'the absurd notion that they are upon a footing with their superiors, in respect of their rights to mental improvement, may be in effect as dangerous to the public peace as the projects of certain revolutionary maniacs'.[1] Such views and such warnings were in the 1820s still commonplace, and against the background of such continuing resistance, and even more of apathy and the haphazard, inadequate provision of schooling, there were reasons for supporting monitorial schemes. Owen's sympathy soon disappeared, however, in his enthusiasm to demonstrate something better. He trained infant teachers who could deal kindly with children. The children themselves, accepted into the school from the age of two or even earlier, were 'trained and educated without punishment or any fear of it'. The instruction he gave his teachers was 'that they were on no account ever to beat any one of the children, or to threaten them in any manner…but were always to speak to them with a pleasant countenance, and in a kind manner and tone of voice'.[2] This was, in the generosity of the provision and the approach, a model of humanitarian education for which there was no parallel.

Adequately to approach the third of our questions—what happened to Owen's ideas—would really require detailed attention to the growth and nature of Owenism, and of other popular social movements which derived at least part of their energy and vision from Owenism. There is no legislation, no organised system of schools, no unfolding pattern of Owenite education in the narrow sense of the word. The chronology of nineteenth-

[1] Quoted in A. D. Lindsay, *The Modern Democratic State* (1962 ed.), p. 135.　　　　[2] See below, pp. 62–4.

century education can only, until 1870 at least, be compiled in terms of what did not happen, or of narrow, sectarian and half-hearted things that did. Owen, battling obstinately for humane objectives, had no institutional influence on a society which now equated progress with production. The policies which governed the institutions of Victorian Britain were not open to the influence of generous systems of thought and action. The context of the late twenties and after was very different from that in which we have seen Owen previously. It will be useful, therefore, to look again at Owen and Owenism after the peak of his success at New Lanark. We need do this only briefly, not because the period is less important than the earlier ones, but because the ideas Owen had arrived at and built into a system did not change. It was the context and the points of pressure that changed.

Owen's active connection with New Lanark declined from 1824, and it ended in 1828–9. William Allen's worries about many aspects of Owen's system of education (for example, the dancing) reached pathological proportions, and Owen had reluctantly to agree to changes. At the same time an opportunity arose to purchase a ready-made village in Indiana, belonging to the Rappite Community of Harmony. Owen bought the 30,000 acres for $150,000, and launched an experiment in community construction that ended—as an Owenite community—in 1827. Between 1824 and 1829 Owen was engaged on what he saw as the practical task of promoting a new, international, social system. It would, he said at New Harmony in 1826, 'spread from Community to Community, from State to State, from Continent to Continent, until this system and these *truths* shall overshadow the whole earth, shedding fragrance and abundance, intelligence and happiness, upon all the sons of men!'.[1] At New Harmony, as throughout his career, Owen was able to command astonishing personal loyalty and to achieve a great deal through his personal influence. It had been true among the New Lanark population and among powerful politicians and church leaders in the 1810s, and it was true among working-class leaders in the 1830s. Here at New Harmony it was equally true. One of his New Harmony followers wrote in June 1825:

I have just returned from hearing Mr. Owen, and I am then always in the hills. I do not know how it is,—he is not an orator; but here he appears to have the power of managing the feelings of all at his will. The day before our arrival here...dissatisfaction prevailed. A day or two after, Mr. Owen spoke, and it vanished.[2]

But the persuasive power of Owen's conviction was not enough, and he was not always present to exercise it. Mistakes were made—some of the most dramatic by Owen himself in his utopian haste; nearly a thousand people flocked into New Harmony, not all in search of ideals; dissensions and divisions were frequent, and in the circumstances inevitable. New Harmony, and his subsequent attempts to promote even larger schemes in the New World, collapsed.

The movements with which he was associated in Britain from 1829 to the end of the Grand National Consolidated Trades Union in 1834 were, unexpectedly for Owen, on a scale to reinforce his hopes of a suitable agency through which his plans would quickly material-

---

[1] Quoted in John Humphrey Noyes, *History of American Social-isms* (1966 ed.), p. 46.
[2] Quoted in Rowland Hill Harvey, *Robert Owen, Social Idealist* (1949), p. 106.

ise. The Owenite cooperative movement, its objectives and activities were in his eyes, to begin with, too small and hopeless a cause, but he played a growing part in its affairs and caught from its working-class leaders some of the conviction that they had derived from him. This movement, it should be emphasised, was a movement to unite for cooperative production, to conduct propaganda activity, and to acquire the means to establish its members in communities on Owenite lines. In all its affairs education was of crucial importance. The cooperative newspapers, the writings of the new generation of Owenite cooperators, and the work of the local cooperative movements all contained a strong commitment to the cause of education. Cooperators founded schools for their children, and organised adult education. To the cooperators and sympathisers Owen was not just the advocate of community and a new way of organising society—he was the apostle of a view of education which reasserted a universal human dignity. Surviving correspondence received by Owen in this period teems with proposals for educational ventures, some of which were begun, some not, and all seeking Owen's expert advice. From a correspondent at Wigan, for example, in 1832:

I have to request your opinion on an undertaking that is of importance to the cooperative system—it is the wish of the cooperative Societies of the North of England . . . to establish a school for 500 children from 4 years old to 14 years . . . and I know your experience will enable you to give us some valuable information on this subject . . .[1]

From 1834 there is correspondence from a couple in Wisbech, 'desirous of obtaining some information from

[1] Co-operative Union Library, Manchester, MS collection, no. 522.

you with regard to the formation of an infant school'. Their intentions are modest, but 'something larger may follow in time'.[1] Throughout this period, and later in his career, numerous organisations and individuals (from penniless cooperators to members of the aristocracy) were anxious to have his educational advice. At a time when change in education was still generally an object of political intrigue and religious manoeuvre, Owen's precept and example had helped considerable sections of the population—and above all the labour movement—to see education, a different form of education, as a serious and desirable objective.

Owen's deep personal involvement in the Labour Exchange and trade union movements took him further into organised social action than he had ever been. The years 1832–4 were for Owen years of crisis and of resolution. For the working class, with its growing sense of identity and exclusion from the central sources of power and justice, the early nineteenth century was a history of crises differing in kind. Luddism, the events that led to Peterloo, and the political reform movement of 1831–2, were part of a scatter of responses to the inhumanities of laissez-faire industrialism, and to the exercise of unrestrained privilege and power. The Reform Act of 1832 left behind a profound resentment at the betrayal of working-class hopes. There were at the same time in some trades—building, for example— deep bewilderments caused by the inability of familiar forms of industrial organisation to maintain standards of living. There were by now strongly established traditions of radical endeavour on behalf of a free Press; there was growing preoccupation with factory conditions, and particularly with the need to restrict working

[1] *Ibid.* no. 785.

hours. Owenism chimed in well with this discontent and provided a focus in organisation and action. The collapse of some of the Owenite ventures, repression in 1834, and the bitterly resisted Poor Law Amendment Act of the same year turned the focus back towards political reform, and Chartism was the next crisis of development. But the working-class crisis of post-Owenism was for Owen the beginning of a New Moral World.

Owenite trade unions and equitable labour exchanges aimed, as did any Owenite movement, at by-passing industrial capitalism. They aimed to produce and to exchange on a basis of rational, communal self-help, and they aimed as much at a new quality of living as they did at intelligent labour organisation. Educational aims, therefore, were built in to the objectives of the trade unions in their Owenite phase. Exchanges were the distributive basis on which education and community were to be possible.

Throughout these years, alongside the exchanges, the cooperative congresses, the trade union activities, a core of Owen's supporters organised, on Owen's own premises, lecturing activities and publications, recreation and schools. Owen himself was active in his Association of the Intelligent and Well Disposed of the Industrious Classes for removing the Causes of Ignorance and Poverty by Education and Employment; he lectured on education, and proclaimed the forthcoming millennium. An Owenite activity anywhere in Britain was inconceivable without lecturing and discussion activities for the adults and at least hopes of a school for the children. The Owenite communities, including for example Orbiston in Scotland, Ralahine in Ireland and Queenwood in Hampshire, were all firmly involved in efforts to provide an imaginative and efficient education for the children.

Chartism, which superseded the Owenism of the early thirties as the main dynamic of popular action, made its primary appeal as a political movement. Involved in it at different stages, however, were far-reaching social objectives. Carlyle, in *Chartism*, sees the answer to wretched conditions and attendant political disturbance as lying partly in education. For six thousand years 'the Sons of Adam, in sleepless effort, have been devising, doing, discovering…warring, a little band of brothers, against the great black empire of Necessity and Night'. But to the uneducated man 'it is all as if it had not been. The four-and-twenty letters of the Alphabet are still Runic enigmas to him.'[1] So Carlyle advocates the dissemination of light. His world is threatened, and partly as an act of justice, partly in self-defence, he wishes to make light available. He is totally unaware, however, of the efforts of Chartists —and of working-class movements widely in the early nineteenth century—to achieve light for themselves. He has underestimated even the extent of working-class literacy.[2]

Chartism produced educational programmes. The founding organ of the movement, the London Working Men's Association, whose leaders were schooled in Owenism, wrote education firmly into its objectives. The educational ideals of some of the Chartist leaders, notably William Lovett, provoked hostility from some of the more militant sections of the movement. But even

[1] *Chartism* (1888 ed.), p. 59.
[2] Indispensable reading on this subject are R. D. Altick, *The English Common Reader* (1957), and R. K. Webb, *The English Working Class Reader* (1955).

while there was disagreement about aims, the work of education proceeded impressively. Chartist Halls, financed by working-class contributions, acted as Chartist meeting centres, and in association with them libraries and schools were frequently to be found.[1] The Christian Chartists of Scotland, for example, established schools which 'were to be connected with the churches and the preacher was to be primarily a teacher 'to elucidate all the principles of the Charter'.[2]

Owen had in the twenties and early thirties offered a vision and a stimulus. Working-class movements had embraced them, and even when they turned from Owenism to political action, Owen's message of education and dignity had become one of the sources of their vigour.

Neither Owen nor Owenism came to a halt in 1834. New generations of Owenites were attracted by its anti-clerical, now explicitly socialist doctrines. Owen created new organisations. Through them, through the Owenite Halls of Science, through the social missionaries who toured the country, through Owen's newspapers, there continued the work of propaganda and education, including in the lecture-room and the school-room.[3] The popular basis of Owenite activity had become severely restricted, but the movement continued with some strength into the 1840s. From then until his death in 1858 Owen continued, a little-heard voice out of the

[1] See Brian Simon, *Studies in the History of Education 1780–1870* (1960), pp. 243–53.
[2] Cowherd, *The Politics of English Dissent*, p. 108 (quoting the *Chartist Circular*).
[3] For this period see Frank Podmore, *Robert Owen*, chs. XIX–XXIII; A. Black, 'Education before Rochdale (2. The Owenites and the Halls of Science)', *Co-operative Review*, XXIX, 2 (1955).

eighteenth century, to assert with inexhaustible energy the message of a rational society. Human qualities, he was explaining to teachers in 1849, 'are *well* or *ill* directed in each individual by *society*'.[1] To 'well-educate', he told them, a 'new mould must be made, in which the new being must be placed from birth', and this mould must include arrangements 'to well-feed, well-clothe, well-lodge, &c., &c., or the education will be defective'.[2] However faulty the education they had in the past been called upon to transmit, and however much 'the teachers require to be taught' (the motto at the head of these *Letters*), he gave to their calling the following testimonial: 'You have hitherto educated the human race;—you will have to continue to educate them; and this is the highest and most important task that man can perform for man.'[3] From outside the institutions of education, therefore, Owen from the 1820s on offered unceasingly a set of criteria by which narrower standards of education could be judged, a vision by which the lack of a proper system could be condemned. The criteria and the vision, it must be repeated, are not measurable in terms of organisational influence. In the 'long revolution' for a more humane education, and a more humane society, other influences were also at work. Across the period of stunted, narrow infant education which followed after Owen in the twenties and thirties—exemplified in Samuel Wilderspin and the London Infant School Society, and the Mayos and the Home and Colonial Infant School Society—there survived, in practice and in texts, relatively humane influences, deriving, for instance,

[1] *Letters on Education*, p. 2.
[2] *Ibid.* p. 10.
[3] *Ibid.* p. 6.

from educators such as David Stow.[1] Pestalozzi and the Continental educators visited by Owen began, after he had made his major impact, to have a following in Britain. In the 1850s in small beginnings, and from the 1870s more widely and effectively, the Froebel movement exercised its influence. Owen was not the least of the contributors to the design of twentieth-century progressivism.

The contribution was not, obviously, only in terms of strictly educational traditions. Owen's contribution to the ideals and activities of the labour movement ran slowly down in the sands of change in the middle of the nineteenth century. But that he had helped effectively to transform the quality of working-class life came to be recognised fully when, in new conditions, the labour movement grappled with a new awakening to the relevance of ideas and ideals. Speaking in Newcastle in 1873, for example, radical Joseph Cowen reminded his audience:

In speaking of co-operation, I think we do not sufficiently recognise the self-sacrificing and self-denying labours of Mr. Owen to spread these principles thirty-five years ago. He threw his bread upon the waters, and it has come back many days hence.[2]

In the new socialist currents of the 1880s further echoes of Owen's views were heard. Annie Besant in 1887 tells how old men still 'dwell fondly on the hopes of the "social missionaries" who were preaching when the men

---

[1] Some of the range of school-room practices, including the humane influence of Stow, can be seen in chapter 6 of Mary Sturt, *The Education of the People* (1967).

[2] Speech on Co-operation, Newcastle, 12 April 1873. In Cowen papers, Newcastle City Reference Library.

37

now of middle age were born'. Some, she says, even remember the experiments of Owen, the hopes raised by New Lanark and Orbiston, and 'the chill disappointment of New Harmony'. Owen's memory had been kept alive in the memories of such men, and in the cooperative movement itself, which 'has prepared men to think of a possible future in which co-operation should wholly replace competition, and Owen's dream of universal brotherhood become a living reality'. Owenite energy had been 'swamped in the sudden rush of prosperity that followed the repeal of the Corn Laws and the English triumph of Free Trade. Now that that rush is long over, and the old misery is on the workers once more, their minds turn back to the old schemes, and they listen readily to suggestions of a new social order.'[1] Owen's experiments failed, 'but... the impulse to seek some rational system of society has, since his time, never quite died out in England'.[2] There followed a renewed interest in and sympathy for Owen's ideals and methods of social analysis. Frank Podmore published his monumental biography of Owen in 1906, and no series on social reformers could escape allocating a prominent place to Owen. In 1908, for example, he was the subject of Joseph Clayton's *Robert Owen: Pioneer of Social Reforms*, and of a chapter in G. R. S. Taylor's *Leaders of Socialism Past and Present*.

Michael Sadler, in 1907, summarised Owen's contribution to education: 'What Robert Owen did for English educational thought was to make some few of his contemporaries perceive the importance of infant

[1] *The Socialist Movement*, p. 4. For references to Owenite energies in the period before the eighties see Royden Harrison, *Before the Socialists* (1965).

[2] *Modern Socialism* (1890, 2nd ed.), p. 7.

schools, and to make many more people realise the inseparable connection between education and the influence of social environment.'[1] Even if that were all, it would be a great deal.

[1] *Owen, Lovett, Maurice, and Toynbee*, p. 8 (reprinted from *The University Review*, July 1907).

# NOTE ON THE TEXTS

Owen lived up to his doctrine that by the assertion of rational views society would be persuaded to behave rationally; most of his writings do in fact assert and reassert similar basic analyses and solutions. It is not surprising that there is a great deal of repetition in his writings as a whole, and even within any given document. In many of the following texts, therefore, sections varying from a few words to a few pages have been cut, either because they are not relevant to the theme of education or because they merely repeat arguments presented elsewhere. The editing, it is hoped, has not distorted the content or blunted the emphases of any of the texts. Punctuation has been left as in the original texts, except for modern treatment of quotation marks. Owen's use of block capitals and italics has been modernised.

Superior figures in the text refer to the Notes, which will be found on pages 216–233.

# THE LIFE OF ROBERT OWEN
## BY HIMSELF

Owen completed only the first volume of his autobiography (published in 1857), covering the period to 1820. The following extracts illustrate aspects of his experience and views up to and including New Lanark.

As it appears in the family great Bible, I was born in Newtown, Montgomeryshire, North Wales, on the 14th of May, 1771, and was baptized on the 12th of June following.

My father was Robert Owen. He was born in Welsh Pool, and was brought up to be a saddler, and probably an ironmonger also, as these two trades were at that period often united in the small towns on the borders of Wales. He married into the family of Williams, a numerous family, who were in my childhood among the most respectable farmers around Newtown.

I think my mother (who was deemed beautiful, as I was informed, when she was married) was the eldest sister of the family, and, for her class, superior in mind and manner.

I suppose that on their marriage they settled in Newtown,—my father taking up his own calling as a saddler and ironmonger. He was also post-master as long as he lived. He had the general management of the parish affairs, being better acquainted, as it appears, with its finances and business, than any other party in the township.

I must have been sent young to school,—probably at between four and five years of age,—for I cannot remember first going there.

In schools in these small towns it was considered a good education if one could read fluently, write a legible hand, and understand the four first rules of arithmetic. And this I have reason to believe was the extent of Mr. Thickness's qualification for a schoolmaster,—because when I had acquired these small rudiments of learning, at the age of seven, he applied to my father for permission that I should become his assistant and usher, as from that time I was called while I remained in school. And thenceforward my schooling was to be repaid by my ushership. As I remained at school about two years longer, those two years were lost to me, except that I thus early acquired the habit of teaching others what I knew.

But at this period I was fond of and had a strong passion for reading everything which fell in my way. As I was known to and knew every family in the town, I had the libraries of the clergyman, physician, and lawyer—the learned men of the town—thrown open to me, with permission to take home any volume which I liked, and I made full use of the liberty given to me.

Among the books which I selected at this period were *Robinson Crusoe*, *Philip Quarle*, *Pilgrim's Progress*, *Paradise Lost*, Harvey's *Meditations among the Tombs*, Young's *Night Thoughts*, Richardson's, and all other standard novels. I believed every word of them to be true, and was therefore deeply interested; and I generally finished a volume daily. Then I read Cook's and all the circumnavigators' voyages,—*The History of the World*,—Rollin's *Ancient History*,—and all the lives I could meet with of the philosophers and great men.

While I remained in Stamford[1] I read upon the average about five hours a day.

One of the entrances to Burleigh Park was near the town; and in summer, and as long as the weather permitted, my chief pleasure was to go early into the park to walk, read, think, and study, in those noble avenues which were then numerous in it. Very often in the midst of summer I was thus in the park from between three and four in the morning until eight, and again in the evening from six or seven until nearly dark. I had transcribed many of Seneca's moral precepts into a book which I kept in my pocket; to ponder over them in the park was one of my pleasurable occupations; and in this park, which I made my study, I read many volumes of the most useful works I could obtain.

I was all this time endeavouring to find out the true religion, and was greatly puzzled for some time by finding all of every sect over the world, of which I read or of which I heard from the pulpits, claim each for themselves to be in possession of the true religion. I studied and studied and carefully compared one with another, for I was very religiously inclined, and desired most anxiously to be in the right way. But the more I heard, read, and reflected, the more I became dissatisfied with Christian, Jew, Mahomedan, Hindoo, Chinese and Pagan. I began seriously to study the foundation of all of them, and to ascertain on what principle they were based. Before my investigations were concluded, I was satisfied that one and all had emanated from the same source, and their varieties from the same false imaginations of our early ancestors. It was with the greatest reluctance, and after long contests in my mind, that I was compelled to abandon my first and deep-rooted impressions in favour of Christianity,—but being obliged to give up my faith in this sect, I was at the same time compelled to reject all others. My own reflections compelled me to come to

43

very different conclusions. My reason taught me that I could not have made one of my own qualities,—that they were forced upon me by Nature;—that my language, religion, and habits, were forced upon me by society; and that I was entirely the child of Nature and Society; —that Nature gave the qualities, and Society directed them. Thus was I forced, through seeing the error of their foundation, to abandon all belief in every religion which had been taught to man. But my religious feelings were immediately replaced by the spirit of universal charity.

About this period[2] cotton spinning was so profitable that it began to engage the attention of many parties with capitals. Mr. Arkwright, the introducer, if not the inventor of the new cotton spinning machinery, had had a cotton spinning mill erected in Manchester; and a Mr. Drinkwater, a rich Manchester manufacturer and foreign merchant, had built a mill for finer spinning, and was beginning to fill it with machinery under the superintendence of a Mr. George Lee, a very superior scientific person in those days. Mr. Lee had given Mr. Drinkwater notice that he must leave him. He had to advertise for a manager to undertake the superintendence of this mill, now in progress; and his advertisement appeared on a Saturday in the Manchester papers, but I had not seen or heard of it until I went to my factory on the Monday morning following, when, as I entered the room where my spinning machines were, one of the spinners said—'Mr. Lee has left Mr. Drinkwater, and he has advertised for a manager.' I merely said—'what will he do?' and passed on to my own occupation. But (and how such an idea could enter my head I know not), without saying a word, I put on my hat and proceeded straight to Mr. Drinkwater's counting-house, and boy, and inexperienced, as I was, I asked him for the situation for which he had advertised. 'What salary do you ask?' 'Three hundred a year'—was my reply. 'What?' Mr Drinkwater said, with some surprise, repeating the words—'Three hundred a year! I have had this morning I know not how many seeking the situation, and I do not think that all their askings together would amount to what you require.' 'I cannot be governed by what others ask,' said I, 'and I cannot take less. I am now making that sum by my own business.' 'Can you prove that to me?' 'Yes, I will show you the business and my books.' 'Then I will go with you, and let me see them,' said Mr. Drinkwater. We went to my factory. I explained the nature of my business, opened the book, and proved my statement to his satisfaction. He then said—'What reference as to past character can you give?' I referred him to Mr. Satterfield, Messrs. Flint and Palmer, and Mr. McGuffog. 'Come to me on such a day, and you shall have my answer.' This was to give him time to make the inquiries.

I called upon him at the time appointed. He said, 'I will give you the three hundred a year, as you ask, and will take all your machinery at its cost price, and I shall require you to take the management of the mill and of the workpeople, about 500, immediately.' Mr. Lee had left the day before I was sent for to take his place, and I entered it without the slightest instruction or explanation about anything. When I arrived at the mill I found myself at once in the midst of five hundred men, women, and children, who were busily occupied with machinery, much of which I had scarcely seen, and never in regular connection to manufacture from the cotton to the finished thread. I said to myself, with feelings I shall never forget,—'How came I here? and how is it possible I can manage these people and this business?' To this period I had been a thoughtful, retiring character, extremely sensitive, and could seldom speak to a stranger without blushing, expecially to one of the other sex, except in the ordinary routine of serving in the departments of business through which I had passed; and I was diffident of my own powers, knowing what a very imperfect and deficient education I had received. I was therefore greatly surprised at myself, that, without thought or reflection, on the impulse of the moment, I had solicited this situation. Had I seen the establishment before I applied to manage it, I should never have thought of doing an act so truly presumptuous. Thus, uninstructed, I had to take the management of the concern.

I at once determined to do the best I could, and began to examine the outline and detail of what was in progress. I looked grave,—inspected everything very minutely,—examined the drawings and calculations of the machinery, as left by Mr. Lee, and these were of great use to me. I was with the first in the morning, and I locked up the premises at night, taking the keys with me. I continued this silent inspection and superintendence day by day for six weeks, saying merely yes or no to the questions of what was to be done or otherwise, and during that period I did not give one direct order about anything. But at the end of that time I felt myself so much master of my position, as to be ready to give directions in every department. I soon perceived the defects in the various processes, and in the correctness which was required in making certain parts of the machinery—all yet in a rude state, compared with the advances which have been made from that time to the present. Mr. Drinkwater found the quality gradually to improve, and the customers for it to prefer the new-made to the old stock. He found also that the people employed were, according to reports made to him by others, well disciplined, and yet well satisfied with the rules, regulations, and mode of management which I had adopted.

I had by this period perceived the constant influence of circumstances over my own proceedings and those of others, and by comparison with myself and others I became conscious of the created differences in our original organizations. Relieved from religious prejudices and their obstructive influences to the attainment of common sense, my mind became simple in its new arrangement of ideas, and gradually came to the conclusion that man could not make his own organization, or any one of its qualities, and that these qualities were, according to their nature, more or less influenced by the circumstances which occurred in the life of each, over which the individual had no other control than these combined circumstances gave him, but over which society had an overwhelming influence; and I therefore viewed human nature in my fellow-creatures through a medium different from others, and with far more charity. My treatment of all with whom I came into communication was so natural, that it generally gained their confidence, and drew forth only their good qualities to me.

In consequence of this to me unconscious power over others—I had produced such effects over the work-people in the factory in the first six months of my management, that I had the most complete influence over them, and their order and discipline exceeded that of any other in or near Manchester; and for regularity and sobriety they were an example which none could then imitate; for the workpeople earned at that period higher wages, and were far more independent than they have ever been since.

I now stood high in the estimation of the Manchester public and of the first Scotch muslin manufacturers, as a maker of fine cotton yarns—the Scotch manufacturers being our chief customers.

At this period there were two institutions which attracted considerable notice in Manchester, and were popular and celebrated each in their way. One was the 'Manchester Literary and Philosophical Society', then under the presidency of the late highly respected Dr. Percival.[3] The other was the 'Manchester College',[4] under Dr. Baines, which after his death was removed to York under Mr. Wellbeloved, and was chiefly for the training of Unitarian ministers.

At this period John Dalton,[5] the Quaker, afterwards the celebrated Dr. Dalton the philosopher, and a Mr. Winstanley, both intimate friends of mine, were assistants in this college under Dr. Baines; and in their room we often met in the evenings and had much and frequent interesting discussions upon religion, morals, and other similar subjects, as well as upon the late discoveries in chemistry and other sciences,—and here Dalton first broached his then undefined atomic theory. We began to think ourselves philosophers. Occasionally we admitted a friend or two to join our circle, but this was considered a favour. At this period Coleridge[6] was studying at one of the universities, and was then considered a genius and eloquent. He solicited permission to join our party, that he might meet me in discussion, as I was the one who opposed the religious prejudices of all sects, though always in a friendly and kind manner, having now imbibed the spirit of charity and kindness for my opponents, which was forced upon me by my knowledge of the true formation of character by nature and society. Mr. Coleridge had a great fluency of words, and he could well put them together in high sounding sentences; but my few words, directly to the point, generally told well; and although the eloquence and learning were with him, the strength of the argument was generally admitted to be on my side.

However heterodox my opinions were, I was solicited to become a member of the 'Literary and Philosophical Society of Manchester', to which I consented. I was thus introduced to the leading professional characters, particularly in the medical profession, which at this period stood high in Manchester, and its leading members were the aristocracy of the town. The manufacturers at this period were generally plodding men of business, with little knowledge and limited ideas, except in their own immediate circle of occupation. The foreign merchants, or rather the merchants in the foreign trade, were somewhat more advanced. Without knowing why, I was thus introduced to the élite of the Manchester Literary and Philosophical Society, for I had not been long a member of the society before I was requested to become a member of its committee, a club which was composed of what were considered the select and most efficient members of the society, and which met always immediately after the regular sittings of the society.

I had now to commence[7] in earnest the great experiment which was to prove to me, by practice, the truth or error of the principles which had been forced on my convictions as everlasting principles of truth, and from which all great and permanent good in practice must proceed—to commence the most important experiment for the happiness of the human race that had yet been instituted at any time in any part of the world. This was, to ascertain whether the character of man could be better formed, and society better constructed and governed, by falsehood, fraud, force, and fear, keeping him in ignorance and slavery to superstition,—or by truth, charity, and love, based on an accurate knowledge of human nature, and by forming all the institutions of society in accordance with that knowledge.

When to my friends and nearest connexions I mentioned that my intentions were to commence a new system of management on principles of justice and kindness, and gradually to abolish punishment in governing the population,—they, one and all, smiled at what they called my simplicity, in imagining I could succeed in such a visionary scheme; and they strongly urged me not to attempt such a hopeless impossibility. My mind, however, was prepared for the task, and to encounter whatever difficulties might arise; and I was much encouraged to proceed by the success which I had experienced with my mode of governing the populations in Mr. Drinkwater's factories.

The population of New Lanark at this period consisted of about 1300, settled in the village as families, and between 400 and 500 pauper children, procured from parishes, whose ages appeared to be from five to ten,—but said to be from seven to twelve. These children were by Mr. Dale's directions well lodged, fed, and clothed, and there was an attempt made to teach them to read, and to teach some of the oldest to write, after the business of the long day was over. But this kind of instruction, when the strength of the children was exhausted, only tormented them, without doing any real good,—for I found that none of them understood anything they attempted to read, and many of them fell asleep during the school hours.

The instructor was a good schoolmaster, on the old mode of teaching, and kind and considerate to the children, but what could he do with 400 or 500 of them under such circumstances? The whole system, although most kindly intended by Mr. Dale, was wretchedly bad, and the establishment had been constructed and managed by ordinary minds, accustomed only to very primitive proceedings. I determined therefore that the engagements respecting the children, made by Mr Dale with the parishes, should run out; that no more pauper children should be received; that the village houses and streets should be improved, and new and better houses erected to receive new families, to supply the place of the pauper children; and that the interior of the mills should be rearranged, and the old machinery replaced by new. But these changes were to be made gradually, and to be effected by the profits of the establishment.

This experiment at New Lanark was the first commencement of practical measures with a view to change the fundamental principle on which society has heretofore been based from the beginning; and no experiment could be more successful in proving the truth of the principle that the character is formed *for* and not *by* the individual.

But I had to commence my experiment, not only in opposition to the disbelief in the truth of the fundamental principle on which I was about to found all my proceedings, but with the strongest prejudices in favour of the truth of the principle which I intended to disprove and overcome. The evil conditions which I had to contend against were the ignorance, superstition, and consequent immoral conduct and bad habits of the great majority of the population; the long day's work which they had to undergo; the inferior qualities and high price of everything which they had to purchase for their own use; the bad arrangements in their houses for rearing and training their children from their birth through infancy and childhood; and their prejudices against an English manufacturer becoming a hard taskmaster, as they imagined I was going to be, because they saw I was going to adopt what they called new-fangled measures.

In addition to these evil conditions around the workpeople, I found it necessary, as the foundation of all future success, to make the establishment not only self-supporting, but also productive of sufficient surplus profits to enable me to effect the changes to the improved conditions which I contemplated. My partners were all commercial men, and expected a profit in addition to interest for their capital. I had therefore to readjust the whole business arrangements, and to make great alterations in the building, and gradually to change the whole machinery of the mills.

The workpeople were systematically opposed to every change which I proposed, and did whatever they could to frustrate my object. For this, as it was natural for them to dislike new measures and all attempts to change their habits, I was prepared, and I made due allowance for these obstructions. My intention was to gain their confidence, and this, from their prejudices to a stranger from a foreign country, as at this time the working class of the Scotch considered England to be, was extremely difficult to attain. My language was naturally different from their Lowland Scotch and the Highland Erse, for they had a large mixture of Highlanders among them. I therefore sought out the individuals who had the most influence among them from their natural powers or position, and to these I took pains to explain what were my intentions for the changes I wished to effect. I explained that they were to procure greater permanent advantages for themselves and their children, and requested that they would aid me in instructing the people, and in preparing them for the new arrangements which I had in contemplation.

By these means I began slowly to make an impression upon some of the least prejudiced and most reasonable among them; but the suspicions of the majority, that I only wanted, as they said, to squeeze as much gain out of them as possible, were long continued. I had great difficulty also in teaching them cleanly habits, and order and system in their proceedings. Yet each year a sensible general improvement was effected.

The retail shops, in all of which spirits were sold, were great nuisances. All the articles sold were bought on credit at high prices, to cover great risks. The qualities were most inferior, and they were retailed out to the workpeople at extravagant rates. I arranged superior stores and shops, from which to supply every article of food, clothing, etc., which they required. I bought everything with money in the first markets, and contracted for fuel, milk, etc., on a large scale, and had the whole of these articles of the best qualities supplied to the people at the cost price. The result of this change was to save them in their expenses full twenty-five per cent., besides giving them the best qualities in everything, instead of the most inferior articles, with which alone they had previously been supplied.

The effects soon became visible in their improved

health and superior dress, and in the general comfort of their houses.

All that I could expect to accomplish at New Lanark, was to ameliorate to some extent the worst evils of a fundamentally erroneous system. Yet, in the estimation of the public, the change which was effected at New Lanark exceeded all expectation. Those strangers who came to scrutinise and examine it, said that the change appeared to them, until they witnessed it, to be utterly impracticable.

I here make these explanations, because the public supposed that I made New Lanark the model of the system which I advocated, and that I wished the world to be composed of such arrangements as New Lanark exhibited in its improved state. Although before I had half accomplished what I ultimately effected there, the improvement in the condition of the workpeople was such that the strangers who visited the works were satisfied; and, compared with all other similarly situated workpeople, these were happy, and publicly expressed their full content with their condition,—still, I knew too well the inferiority of their mind and condition, and the injustice they were yet suffering, to be satisfied for them, —knowing how much more society could beneficially do for them, and for all other classes.

Let it therefore be kept in everlasting remembrance, that that which I effected at New Lanark was only the best I could accomplish under the circumstances of an ill-arranged manufactory and village, which existed before I undertook the government of the establishment.

In searching out the evil conditions in which the workpeople were involved, their domestic arrangements for rearing their children from infancy appeared to me especially to be injurious to parents and children.

The houses of the poor and working classes generally are altogether unfit for the training of young children, who, under the limited space and accommodations of these dwellings, are always in the way of their parents, who must be occupied about their daily affairs; the children are therefore spoken to and treated just the reverse of the manner required to well-train and well-educate children. And in ninety-nine cases out of a hundred, parents are altogether ignorant of the right method of treating children, and their own children especially. These considerations created in me the first thoughts respecting the necessity of an infant school, to be based on the true principle of forming character from the earliest period at which the infants could leave their parents.

These children were now surrounded by evil conditions. I wished to take them, as much as our establishment could be made to admit, out of those evil conditions, and to place them within better conditions for forming their tempers and habits. I was surrounded with difficulties to oppose the carrying of my views into practice. To erect and finish a building for my purpose would require an expenditure in the first instance of about five thousand pounds,—and a considerable annual outlay afterwards. But this I estimated would gradually be amply repaid by the improved character of the children, and the improved condition of the parents. I had then, when the building should be erected, to overcome the prejudices of the parents against sending their children so young to school. I had to meet the objections of my partners, who were all good commercial men, and looked to the main chance, as they termed it,—which was a good return for their capital. And I was opposed in all my views by the parish minister. In contemplating this new measure, my mind led me to the necessity for making arrangements to well-form the character of the rising population of New Lanark from the earliest period to maturity, as far as a cotton-spinning establishment could be made to effect it, and commercial men to agree to it. I therefore laid the plan as deep and wide for this purpose as the means under my control would admit.

My mind had been early deeply impressed while in Manchester with the importance of education for the human race. I had watched and aided the progress of Lancaster[8] in his early attempts to commence something towards a beginning to instruct the poor, and had encouraged him to the extent that my means permitted. And when the Church set up Dr. Bell[9] in opposition to Lancaster, I was inclined equally to encourage Dr. Bell.

I immediately perceived the fundamental error of both Church and Dissent; but the beginning of some education, however defective, was much better than the entire neglect of it; and I confidently expected that when once commenced it would gradually progress towards a much more matured state. I therefore assisted Lancaster, from first to last, with a thousand pounds, and offered to Dr. Bell's committee a like amount, if they would open the national schools to children of parents of every creed; but I offered to give them only half the sum if they persisted in their rule to shut the doors against all except those professing the creed of the Church of England. The committee of the national schools debated this proposal of mine for two days, and at length decided, by a small majority of votes, as I was informed, to receive the five hundred pounds, keeping their doors closed againt Dissent; and declined to open them for a gift of double the amount. I thus saved my five hundred pounds, and I had the satisfaction to learn that the result of those two debates was to cause the doors of the national schools to be opened to Dissent in about twelve months afterwards.

I began in 1809 to clear the foundation for the infant and other schools, to form the new character of the rising population; but until the first of January 1816 I was prevented carying my scheme into actual practice.

I had by this time (1809) made such progress in training the people in better and more sober and industrious habits, and in discovering the capacity of the establishment for more extended operations, that I recommended to my partners in London and Manchester the advantages that might be derived by the changes and reforms which I advocated. The statements which I made to them went beyond their views and alarmed them by their extent. The leading partners from each house came from London and Manchester to see what I had done and was doing. Some of the parties were timid, and were afraid to agree to my extended recommendations; and after some months' consideration, some more of the acting and principal partners came again to hear the full outline and detail of that which I proposed to do.

I explained to them my intended measures, step by step, and stated the beneficial effects which I expected they would produce.

Seeing the dilemma in which they appeared to be, I said, 'If you are afraid to proceed with me, I will offer you a sum for the establishment, which I will either give for it, or accept from you, and in the latter case the establishment shall be yours and under your own control.' The reply was, 'Your offer is fair and liberal. What is the sum you fix as its value?' I said, 'Eighty-four thousand pounds.' After some short conversation among themselves they replied, 'We accept your offer, and the establishment is yours.' I thus for the second time[10] fixed the price for these mills.

I went to London[11] sometime before the sale, to see to the printing and publishing of four essays which I had written on the formation of character, and my partners supposed I was occupied only with such public measures, and with the parties who were engaged with myself in promoting means to forward Dr. Bell's and Mr. Lancaster's plans for educating the poor, and in other public matters which were then beginning to occupy the attention of benevolent men, for this was at the commencement of the new era for ameliorating the condition of the poor, and for educating their children,—and during this year (1813) I was thus much occupied.

I was, however, also engaged in forming a new partnership for carrying forward the establishment at New Lanark. I was completely tired of partners who were merely trained to buy cheap and sell dear.

I at this time published a pamphlet for private circulation, stating the preparation which I had made to conduct the establishment at New Lanark on principles to ensure the improvement of the condition of the people as well as to obtain a reasonable remuneration for capital and for its management. These were circulated among the best circles of the wealthy benevolent, and of those who desired with sincerity to commence active measures for the improvement of the condition of the poor and working classes; with a view of obtaining among them partners who would assist, and not retard, my intended future operations, and who would not exact from those they employed too much labour for too little wages. Such partners[12] I found, possessing these views to a greater extent than I had anticipated, in Mr. John Walker, of Arno's Grove; Jeremy Bentham, the philosopher; Joseph Foster of Bromley; William Allen of Plough Court; Joseph Fox, dentist; and Michael Gibbs, subsequently Alderman and Lord Mayor of London—all of whom were willing to become partners with me if the establishment could be bought at a fair price at the sale.

By this period of my life (from 1810 to 1815), my four *Essays on the Formation of Character*, and my practice at New Lanark, had made me well known among the leading men of that period.[13] Among these were the Archbishop of Canterbury,—the Bishop of London, afterwards Archbishop of Canterbury,—Burgess, Bishop of St. David's,—Mr. Wilberforce,—W. Godwin,—Thomas Clarkson,—Zachary Macaulay,—Mr. Thornton, banker, —William Allen,—Joseph Foster,—Hoare, senr., banker,—the first Sir Robert Peel,—Sir Thomas Bernard and his particular friend the Bishop of Durham, Barrington,—the Rev. William Turner of Newcastle,— Mr. Wellbeloved, Principal of the Manchester College in York,—the Bishop of Peterborough,—and many others whose names have faded from society, and many whom I have forgotten. But I must not forget my friends of the political economists—Messrs. Malthus, James Mill, Ricardo, Sir James Macintosh, Colonel Torrens, Francis Place, etc., etc. From these political economists, often in animated discussions, I always differed. But our discussions were maintained to the last with great good feeling and a cordial friendship. They were liberal men for their time; friends to the national education of the people, but opposed to national employment for the poor and unemployed, or to the greatest creation of real wealth,—which surprised me in men who professed to desire the greatest amount of wealth to be produced, but which could only be effected by the well-directed industry at all times of all.

Knowing and feeling as I did the all-importance of education for the mass, as a preliminary to the ultimate true formation of character, I was so profuse or extravagant, as I have stated, in my encouragement of Joseph Lancaster and Dr. Bell, in their measures to make a beginning in this country to give even the mite of instruction to the poor which their respective systems proposed to do, because I trusted that a beginning might be made to lead on gradually to something substantial and permanently beneficial to society.

My next move in this direction was to encourage Lancaster to come to Scotland (where the new manufacturing system was involving the children of the working classes in new conditions, unfavourable to knowledge, to health, and to happiness), to create a public opinion to assist to counteract these evils. He came to Glasgow in 1812, and a great public dinner was to be given to introduce him into Scotland, as a great friend to the instruction of the poor on a new invented economical plan, by which one man could instruct a thousand children.

Joseph Lancaster was now becoming well known and celebrated for this mechanical invention and instruction, and his arrival in Glasgow created much excitement among the friends to the education of the poor. Lancaster, knowing that I was acquainted with the peculiar customs and religious prejudices of the Society of Friends, of which he was a member, made it a special condition, before he could consent as a Quaker to attend a public dinner for his reception into Scotland, that I would consent to be its chairman.

It was on announcing the object of the meeting in my opening speech[14] that I first declared in public my sentiments on the true formation of character, and my principle that man was essentially the creature of the circumstances or conditions in which he was placed, and that I advocated the necessity for preparing measures to place the rising generation within good and superior circumstances. The whole assembly became far more enthusiastic in their continued applause when I concluded, than I ever witnessed in a Scotch audience.

This spontaneous approval by the numerous literary parties present, and the reception given to Joseph Lancaster, induced me to write my first four essays on *A New View of Society*, and on the formation of character. The first two essays were published at the end of this year (1812), and the last two in the beginning of 1813.

In all my projected improvements for educating and improving the condition of the children and workpeople of New Lanark, I had no coadjutors in my near connexions, partners, or friends, until I formed my last partnership in 1814. Previously one and all connected with and around me, except Mr. Dale while he lived, opposed my views with all the arguments they could muster against them; and I lost two sets of partners by persevering in what they called my visionary plans. But when I published these four essays on the formation of character, explanatory of the principles and practices on which I had been acting, I was surprised at the manner in which they were received by the public, and especially by the higher members of the then administration and of the churches; for the heads of both[15] were most anxious to see them previous to their publication.

I had been and was making great and substantial progress with my New Lanark experiment, and it was now becoming widely known, and attracted the attention of those in advanced stations at home and abroad. I had now completed, and furnished according to my new mode of instruction by sensible signs and familiar conversation, the first institution for the formation of the infant and child character—the infants being received into it at one year old, or as soon as they could walk.

The parents at first could not understand what I was going to do with their little children at *two* years of age, but seeing the results produced they became eager to send their infants at one year old, and inquired if I could not take them yet younger.

I charged the parents, that it might not be considered a pauper school, threepence per month, or three shillings a year, for each child, and of course they paid this most willingly. The expense of this establishment of three gradations of schools was about two pounds per year for each child. But the difference between the three shillings and two pounds was amply made up by the improved character of the whole population, upon whom the school had a powerful influence for good.

The children were trained and educated without punishment or any fear of it, and were while in school by far the happiest human beings I have ever seen.

The infants and young children, besides being instructed by sensible signs,—the things themselves, or models or paintings,—and by familiar conversation, were from two years and upwards daily taught dancing and singing, and the parents were encouraged to come and see their children at any of their lessons or physical exercises.

But in addition there were day schools for all under

twelve years old, after which age they might, if their parents wished, enter the works.

I had before this period acquired the most sincere affections of all the children. I had also the hearts of all their parents, who were highly delighted with the improved conduct, extraordinary progress, and continually increasing happiness of their children, and with the substantial improvements by which I gradually surrounded them. But the great attraction to myself and the numerous strangers who now continually visited the establishment, was the new infant school; the progress of which from its opening I daily watched and superintended, until I could prepare the mind of the master whom I had selected for this, in my estimation, most important charge,—knowing that if the foundation were not truly laid, it would be in vain to expect a satisfactory structure.

It was in vain to look to any old teachers upon the old system of instruction by books. In the previous old schoolroom I had tried to induce the master to adopt my views; but he could not and would not attempt to adopt what he deemed to be such a fanciful 'new-fangled' mode of teaching, and he was completely under the influence of the minister of the parish, who was himself also opposed to any change of system in teaching children, and who considered that the attempt to educate and teach infants was altogether a senseless and vain proceeding. I had therefore, although he was a good obstinate 'dominie' of the old school, reluctantly to part with him, and I had to seek among the population for two persons who had a great love for and unlimited patience with infants, and who were thoroughly tractable and willing unreservedly to follow my instructions. The best to my mind in these respects that I could find in the population of the village, was a poor simple-hearted weaver, named James Buchanan,[16] who had been previously trained by his wife to perfect submission to her will, and who could gain but a scanty living by his now dying trade of weaving common plain cotton goods by hand. But he loved children strongly by nature, and his patience with them was inexhaustible. These, with his willingness to be instructed, were the qualities which I required in the master for the first rational infant school that had ever been imagined by any party in any country.

But infants so young, also required a female nurse, to assist the master, and one also who possessed the same natural qualifications. Such an one I found among the numerous young females employed in the cotton mills, and I was fortunate in finding for this task a young woman, about seventeen years of age, known familiarly among the villagers as 'Molly Young', who of the two, in natural powers of mind, had the advantage over her new companion in an office perfectly new to both.

The first instruction which I gave them was, that they were on no account ever to beat any one of the children, or to threaten them in any manner in word or action, or to use abusive terms; but were always to speak to them with a pleasant countenance, and in a kind manner and tone of voice. That they should tell the infants and children (for they had all from one to six years old under their charge) that they must on all occasions do all they could to make their playfellows happy,—and that the older ones, from four to six years of age, should take especial care of younger ones, and should assist to teach them to make each other happy.

These instructions were readily received by James Buchanan and Molly Young, and were faithfully adhered to by them as long as they remained in their respective situations.

The children were not to be annoyed with books; but were to be taught the uses and nature or qualities of the common things around them, by familiar conversation when the children's curiosity was excited so as to induce them to ask questions respecting them.

From this rational infant school have arisen all the unsuccessful attempts[17] to form a second with similar results.

The second attempt to form one was made by the Marquis of Lansdowne, Lord Brougham,[18] John Smith, banker, M.P.; Benjamin Smith, M.P.; Henry Hase, Esq., cashier of the Bank of England; and, I believe, James Mill, afterwards of the India House. Lord Brougham, John Smith, and Henry Hase had frequently visited New Lanark and enjoyed the goodness, happiness, and intelligence of the children in these rational surroundings, constituting the institution for the formation of this new character; and being benevolent men, they naturally desired that so much goodness and happiness should be if possible extended to all other poor children. They asked me whether, if they could form a party to establish one in London, I would give them James Buchanan to be the master of their school. I replied—'Most willingly, for I have pupils who can take his place without any injury to my school.'

I had thought, from the daily instruction which, when at the establishment I had as it were drilled into him for years, that he could now act from himself in a practice which under my direction, with the aid he received from Molly Young, appeared so easy to execute. But I found he could proceed no further in the practice than he had done for some time.

The gentlemen named formed a party to carry the proposed scheme into practice, and a school was erected and furnished, and James Buchanan and his family went to London, and he was appointed master, with full powers over the school.

I now had to appoint and instruct a successor to James Buchanan, and soon one of the new trained pupils, who had passed through our schools, and who was therefore much in advance of his former master as a scholar and in habits, became greatly his superior, and by his youth and vigour, aided by a fine enthusiasm in the cause, which I had been enabled to create in him, a rapid advance and improvement were made in the first year after James Buchanan had left the school, and he, James Buchanan, never afterwards saw it.

Now I expected he would have had his new school in Westminster equal to the one he had been so much accustomed to for so long a period. But though he was a willing servant, to attend to the instructions given to him, as far as his good-natured limited powers would admit, it proved that he had neither mind nor energy to act for himself. It was some time after this second school was established and in full action, before I could leave New Lanark, having to train my new young master to direct the infant school in my absence. This young man had been systematically trained through our three schools in the institution for forming character, and his character had been well formed. He had imbibed the true spirit of the system, and was eager to be taught the means to carry the improvements which I wished into practice. He was full of faculty for the employment, and at sixteen years of age was the best instructor of infants I have ever seen in any part of the world.

While these matters were in progress at New Lanark, the fame of its infant school and of the institution for the formation of character was noised abroad and created much excitement, and travellers of distinction, home and foreign, came increasingly year by year to see what they called the wonders of New Lanark.

Knowing that inspection alone could give any adequate impression of the results produced here, I freely opened the whole establishment to the full investigation of all comers. I said to the public—'Come and see, and judge for yourselves.' And the public came—not by hundreds, but by thousands annually.

# A NEW VIEW OF SOCIETY

*or, Essays on the Formation of the Human Character
Preparatory to the Development of a Plan for gradually
ameliorating the Condition of Mankind*

A note in the first edition explains: 'The First Essay was
written in 1812, and published early in 1813. The Second
Essay was written and published at the end of 1813...They
were first printed for sale in July 1816.' Slight cuts have been
made in the second essay, and heavier ones in the third and
fourth. The dedicatory addresses have been omitted.

## ESSAY FIRST

According to the last returns under the Population Act,
the poor and working classes of Great Britain and Ireland have been found to exceed twelve millions of
persons, or nearly three fourths of the population of the
British Islands.

The characters of these persons are now permitted to
be very generally formed without proper guidance or
direction, and, in many cases, under circumstances
which directly impel them to a course of extreme vice
and misery; thus rendering them the worst and most
dangerous subjects in the empire; while the far greater
part of the remainder of the community are educated
upon the most mistaken principles of human nature,
such indeed as cannot fail to produce a general conduct
throughout society totally unworthy of the character of
rational beings.

The first thus unhappily situated are the poor and
the uneducated profligate among the working classes,

who are now trained to commit crimes, for the commission of which they are afterwards punished.

The second is the remaining mass of the population, who are now instructed to believe, or at least to acknowledge, that certain principles are unerringly true, and to act as though they were grossly false; thus filling the world with folly and inconsistency, and making society, throughout all its ramifications, a scene of insincerity and counteraction.

In this state the world has continued to the present time; its evils have been and are continually increasing; they cry aloud for efficient corrective measures, which if we longer delay, general disorder must ensue.

'But', say those who have not deeply investigated the subject, 'attempts to apply remedies have been often made, yet all of them have failed. The evil is now of a magnitude not to be controlled; the torrent is already too strong to be stemmed; and we can only wait with fear or calm resignation, to see it carry destruction in its course by confounding all distinctions of right and wrong.'

Such is the language now held, and such are the general feelings on this most important subject.

These, however, if longer suffered to continue, must lead to the most lamentable consequences. Rather than pursue such a course, the character of legislators would be infinitely raised, if, forgetting the petty and humiliating contentions of sects and parties, they would thoroughly investigate the subject, and endeavour to arrest and overcome these mighty evils.

The chief object of these Essays is to assist and forward investigations of such vital importance to the well-being of this country, and of society in general.

The view of the subject which is about to be given

has arisen from extensive experience for upwards of twenty years, during which period its truth and importance have been proved by multiplied experiments. That the writer may not be charged with precipitation or presumption, he has had the principle and its consequences, examined, scrutinized, and fully canvassed by some of the most learned, intelligent, and competent characters of the present day; who on every principle of duty as well as of interest, if they had discovered error in either would have exposed it;—but who, on the contrary, have fairly acknowledged their incontrovertible truth and practical importance.

Assured, therefore, that his principles are true, he proceeds with confidence, and courts the most ample and free discussion of the subject; courts it for the sake of humanity—for the sake of his fellow creatures—millions of whom experience sufferings, which, were they to be unfolded, would compel those who govern the world to exclaim, 'Can these things exist and we have no knowledge of them?' But they do exist—and even the heart-rending statements which were made known to the public during the discussions upon negro-slavery, do not exhibit more afflicting scenes than those which, in various parts of the world, daily arise from the injustice of society towards itself; from the inattention of mankind to the circumstances which incessantly surround them, and from the want of a correct knowledge of human nature in those who govern and control the affairs of men.

If these circumstances did not exist to an extent almost incredible, it would be unnecessary now to contend for a principle regarding Man, which scarcely requires more than to be fairly stated to make it self-evident.

This principle is, that 'Any general character, from the best to the worst, from the most ignorant to the most enlightened, may be given to any community, even to the world at large, by the application of proper means; which means are to a great extent at the command and under the control of those who have influence in the affairs of men.'

The principle as now stated is a broad one, and, if it should be found to be true, cannot fail to give a new character to legislative proceedings, and such a character as will be most favourable to the well-being of society.

That this principle is true to the utmost limit of the terms, is evident from the experience of all past ages and from every existing fact.

Shall misery, then, most complicated and extensive, be experienced, from the prince to the peasant, throughout all the nations of the world, and shall its cause, and the means of its prevention, be known, and yet these means withheld? The undertaking is replete with difficulties, which can only be overcome by those who have influence in society; who, by foreseeing its important practical benefits, may be induced to contend against those difficulties; and who, when its advantages are clearly seen and strongly felt, will not suffer individual considerations to be put in competition with their attainment. It is true their ease and comfort may be for a time sacrificed to those prejudices; but, if they persevere, the principles on which this knowledge is founded must ultimately universally prevail.

In preparing the way for the introduction of these principles, it cannot now be necessary to enter into the detail of facts to prove that children can be trained to acquire 'any language, sentiments, belief, or any bodily habits and manners, not contrary to human nature'.

For that this has been done, the history of every nation of which we have records abundantly confirms; and that this is, and may be again done, the facts which exist around us and throughout all the countries in the world prove to demonstration.

Possessing then the knowledge of a power so important; which, when understood, is capable of being wielded with the certainty of a law of nature, and which would gradually remove the evils which now chiefly afflict mankind, shall we permit it to remain dormant and useless, and suffer the plagues of society perpetually to exist and increase?

No: the time is now arrived when the public mind of this country and the general state of the world call imperatively for the introduction of this all-pervading principle, not only in theory, but into practice.

Nor can any human power now impede its rapid progress. Silence will not retard its course, and opposition will give increased celerity to its movements. The commencement of the work will, in fact, ensure its accomplishment; henceforth all the irritating, angry passions, arising from ignorance of the true cause of bodily and mental character, will gradually subside, and be replaced by the most frank and conciliating confidence and good-will.

Nor will it be possible hereafter for comparatively a few individuals, unintentionally to occasion the rest of mankind to be surrounded by circumstances which inevitably form such characters, as they afterwards deem it a duty and a right to punish even to death; and that too, while they themselves have been the instruments of forming those characters. Such proceedings not only create innumerable evils to the directing few, but essentially retard them and the great mass of society from attaining the enjoyment of a high degree of positive happiness. Instead of punishing crimes after they have permitted the human character to be formed so as to commit them, they will adopt the only means which can be adopted to prevent the existence of those crimes; means by which they may be most easily prevented.

Happily for poor traduced and degraded human nature, the principle for which we now contend will speedily divest it of all the ridiculous and absurd mystery with which it has been hitherto enveloped by the ignorance of preceding times: and all the complicated and counteracting motives for good conduct, which have been multiplied almost to infinity, will be reduced to one single principle of action, which, by its evident operation and sufficiency, shall render this intricate system unnecessary, and ultimately supersede it in all parts of the earth. That principle is the happiness of self clearly understood and uniformly practised; which can only be attained by conduct that must promote the happiness of the community.

For that Power which governs and pervades the universe has evidently so formed man, that he must progressively pass from a state of ignorance to intelligence, the limits of which it is not for man himself to define; and in that progress to discover, that his individual happiness can be increased and extended only in proportion as he actively endeavours to increase and extend the happiness of all around him. The principle admits neither of exclusion nor of limitation; and such appears evidently the state of the public mind that it will now seize and cherish this principle as the most precious boon which it has yet been allowed to attain. The errors of all opposing motives will appear in their true light and the ignorance whence they arose will become so glaring that even the most unenlightened will speedily reject them.

For this state of matters, and for all the gradual changes contemplated, the extraordinary events of the present times have essentially contributed to prepare the way.

Even the late Ruler of France,[19] although immediately influenced by the most mistaken principles of ambition, has contributed to this happy result, by shaking to its foundation that mass of superstition and bigotry, which on the continent of Europe had been accumulating for ages, until it had so overpowered and depressed the human intellect, that to attempt improvement without its removal would have been most unavailing. And, in the next place, by carrying the mistaken selfish principles in which mankind have been hitherto educated to the extreme in practice, he has rendered their error manifest, and left no doubt of the fallacy of the source whence they originated.

These transactions in which millions have been immolated, or consigned to poverty and bereft of friends, will be preserved in the records of time, and impress future ages with a just estimation of the principles now about to be introduced into practice; and will thus prove perpetually useful to all succeeding generations.

For the direful effects of Napoleon's government have created the most deep-rooted disgust at notions which could produce a belief that such conduct was glorious, or calculated to increase the happiness of even the individual by whom it was pursued.

And the late discoveries, and proceedings of the Rev. Dr. Bell and Mr. Joseph Lancaster, have also been preparing the way in a manner the most opposite, but yet not less effectual, by directing the public attention to the beneficial effects, on the young and unresisting mind, of even the limited education which their systems embrace.

They have already effected enough to prove that all which is now in contemplation respecting the training of youth may be accomplished without fear of disappointment. And by so doing, as the consequences of their improvements cannot be confined within the British Isles, they will for ever be ranked among the most important benefactors of the human race. But henceforward to contend for any new exclusive system will be in vain: the public mind is already too well informed, and has too far passed the possibility of retrogression, much longer to permit the continuance of any such evil.

For it is now obvious that such a system must be destructive of the happiness of the excluded, by their seeing others enjoy what they are not permitted to possess; and also that it tends, by creating opposition from the justly injured feelings of the excluded, in proportion to the extent of the exclusion, to diminish the happiness even of the privileged: the former therefore can have no rational motive for its continuance. If however, owing to the irrational principles by which the world has been hitherto governed, individuals, or sects, or parties, shall yet by their plans of exclusion attempt to retard the amelioration of society, and prevent the introduction into practice of that truly just spirit which knows no exclusion, such facts shall yet be brought forward as cannot fail to render all their efforts vain. It will therefore be the essence of wisdom in the privileged classes to co-operate sincerely and cordially with those who desire not to touch one iota of the supposed advantages which they now possess; and whose first and last wish is to increase the particular happiness of those classes as well as the general happiness of society. A very little reflection on the part of the privileged will insure this line of conduct; whence, without domestic revolution[20]—without war and bloodshed— nay, without prematurely disturbing any thing which exists, the world will be prepared to receive principles which are alone calculated to build up a system of happiness, and to destroy those irritable feelings which have so long afflicted society,—solely because society has hitherto been ignorant of the true means by which the most useful and valuable character may be formed.

This ignorance being removed, experience will soon teach us how to form character, individually and generally, so as to give the greatest sum of happiness to the individual, and to mankind.

These principles require only to be known in order to establish themselves: the outline of our future proceedings then becomes clear and defined, nor will they permit us henceforth to wander from the right path. They direct that the governing powers of all countries should establish rational plans for the education and general formation of the characters of their subjects.— These plans must be devised to train children from their earliest infancy in good habits of every description (which will of course prevent them from acquiring those of falsehood and deception). They must afterwards be rationally educated, and their labour be usefully directed. Such habits and education will impress them with an active and ardent desire to promote the happiness of every individual, and that without the shadow of exception for sect, or party, or country, or climate. They will also insure, with the fewest possible exceptions, health, strength, and vigour of body; for the happiness of man can be erected only on the foundations of health of body and peace of mind.

And that health of body and peace of mind may be preserved sound and entire, through youth and manhood, to old age, it becomes equally necessary that the irresistible propensities which form part of his nature, and which now produce the endless and ever multiplying evils with which humanity is afflicted, should be so directed as to increase and not to counteract his happiness.

The knowledge however thus introduced will make it evident to the understanding, that by far the greater part of the misery with which man is encircled may be easily dissipated and removed; and that with mathematical precision he may be surrounded with those circumstances which must gradually increase his happiness.

Hereafter, when the public at large shall be satisfied that these principles can and will withstand the ordeal through which they must inevitably pass; when they shall prove themselves true to the clear comprehension and certain conviction of the unenlightened as well as the learned; and when by the irresistible power of truth, detached from falsehood, they shall establish themselves in the mind, no more to be removed but by the entire annihilation of the human intellects; then the consequent practice which they direct shall be explained, and rendered easy of adoption.

In the mean time, let no one anticipate evil, even in the slightest degree, from these principles; they are, not innoxious only, but pregnant with consequences to be wished and desired beyond all others by every individual in society.

Some of the best intentioned among the various classes in society may still say, 'All this is very delightful and very beautiful in theory, but visionaries alone can expect to see it realized.' To this remark only one reply can or ought to be made; that these principles have been carried most successfully into practice. The present Essays therefore are not brought forward as mere matter of speculation, to amuse the idle visionary who thinks in his closet and never acts in the world; but to create universal activity, pervade society with a knowledge of its true interests, and direct the public mind to the most important object to which it can be directed; to a national proceeding for rationally forming the characters of that immense mass of population which is now allowed to be so formed as to fill the world with crimes. Shall questions of merely local and temporary interest, whose ultimate results are calculated only to withdraw pecuniary profits from one set of individuals and give them to others, engage day after day the attention of politicians and ministers; call forth petitions and delegates from the widely spread agricultural and commercial interests of the empire;—and shall the well-being of millions of the poor, half-naked, half-famished, untaught and untrained, hourly increasing to a most alarming extent in these islands, not call forth one petition, one delegate, or one rational effective legislative measure? No! for such has been our education, that we hesitate not to devote years and expend millions in the detection and punishment of crimes, and in the attainment of objects whose ultimate results are in comparison with this insignificancy itself; and yet we have not moved one step in the true path to prevent crimes, and to diminish the innumerable evils with which mankind are now afflicted. Are these false principles of conduct in those who govern the world to influence mankind permanently,—and if not, how and when is the change to commence? These important considerations shall form the subject of the next essay.

SECOND ESSAY

*The Principles of the Former Essay*
*continued and applied in part to Practice*

General principles only were developed in the First Essay. In this an attempt will be made to show the advantages which may be derived from the adoption of those principles into practice, and to explain the mode by which the practice may without inconvenience be generally introduced.

Some of the most important benefits to be derived from the introduction of those principles into practice are, that they will create the most cogent reasons to induce each man 'to have charity for *all* men'. No feeling short of this can indeed find place in any mind which has been taught clearly to understand, that children in all parts of the earth have been, are, and everlastingly will be impressed with habits and sentiments similar to those of their parents and instructors; modified, however, by the circumstances in which they have been, are, or may be placed, and by the peculiar original organization of each individual. Yet not one of these causes of character is at the command, or in any manner under the control, of infants, who (whatever absurdity we may have been taught to the contrary) cannot possibly be accountable for the sentiments and manners which may be given to them. And here lies the fundamental error of society, and from hence have

79

proceeded, and do proceed, most of the miseries of mankind.

Children are, without exception, passive and wonderfully contrived compounds; which, by an accurate previous and subsequent attention, founded on a correct knowledge of the subject, may be formed collectively to have any human character. And although these compounds, like all the other works of nature, possess endless varieties, yet they partake of that plastic quality, which, by perseverance under judicious management, may be ultimately moulded into the very image of rational wishes and desires.

In the next place, these principles cannot fail to create feelings, which without force, or the production of any counteracting motive, will irresistibly lead those who possess them to make due allowance for the difference of sentiments and manners, not only among their friends and countrymen, but also among the inhabitants of every region of the earth, even including their enemies. With this insight into the formation of character, there is no conceivable foundation for private displeasure or public enmity. Say, if it be within the sphere of possibility that children can be trained to attain that knowledge, and at the same time to acquire feelings of enmity towards a single human creature? The child who from infancy has been rationally instructed in these principles, will readily discover and trace whence the opinions and habits of his associates have arisen, and why they possess them. At the same age he will have acquired reasons sufficient to exhibit to him forcibly the irrationality of being angry with an individual for possessing qualities which, as a passive being during the formation of those qualities, he had not the means of preventing. Such are the impressions these principles will make on the mind of every child so taught; and instead of generating anger or displeasure, they will produce commiseration and pity for those individuals who possess either habits or sentiments which appear to him to be destructive of their own comfort, pleasure, or happiness; and will produce on his part a desire to remove those causes of distress, that his own feelings of commiseration and pity may be also removed. The pleasure which he cannot avoid experiencing by this mode of conduct will likewise stimulate him to the most active endeavours to withdraw those circumstances which surround any part of mankind with causes of misery, and to replace them with others which have a tendency to increase happiness. He will then also strongly entertain the desire to 'do good to *all* men', and even to those who think themselves his enemies.

Thus shortly, directly, and certainly may mankind be taught the essence, and to attain the ultimate object, of all former moral and religious instruction.

These essays, however, are intended to explain that which is true, and not to attack that which is false. For to explain that which is true may permanently improve, without creating even temporary evil; whereas to attack that which is false, is often productive of very fatal consequences. The former convinces the judgement, when the mind possesses full and deliberative powers of judging; the latter instantly arouses irritation, and renders the judgement unfit for its office, and useless. But why should we ever irritate? Do not these principles make it so obvious as to place it beyond any doubt, that even the present irrational ideas and practices prevalent throughout the world, are not to be charged as either a fault or culpable error of the existing generation? The immediate cause of them was the partial ignorance of our forefathers, who, although they acquired some vague disjointed knowledge of the principles on which character is formed, could not discover the connected chain of those principles, and consequently knew not how to apply them to practice. They taught their children that which they had themselves been taught, that which they had acquired; and in so doing they acted like their forefathers; who retained the established customs of former generations until better and superior were discovered and made evident to them.

The present race of men have also instructed their children as they had been previously instructed, and are equally unblameable for any defects which their systems contain. And however erroneous or injurious that instruction and those systems may now be proved to be, the principles on which these essays are founded will be misunderstood, and their spirit will be wholly misconceived, if either irritation, or the slightest degree of ill will, shall be generated against those who even tenaciously adhere to the worst parts of that instruction, and support the most pernicious of those systems. For such individuals, sects, or parties have been trained from infancy to consider it their duty and interest so to act, and in so acting they merely continue the customs of their predecessors. Let truth unaccompanied with error be placed before them; give them time to examine it, and see that it is in unison with all previously ascertained truths, and conviction and acknowledgement of it will follow of course. It is weakness itself to require assent before conviction, and afterwards it will not be withheld. To endeavour to force conclusions, without making the subject clear to the understanding, is most unjustifiable and irrational, and must prove useless or injurious to the mental faculties. In the spirit thus described we therefore proceed in the investigation of the subject.

The facts which by the invention of printing have gradually accumulated, now show the errors of the systems of our forefathers so distinctly, that they must be, when pointed out, evident to all classes of the community, and render it absolutely necessary that new legislative measures be immediately adopted, to prevent the confusion which must arise from even the most ignorant being competent to detect the absurdity and glaring injustice of many of those laws by which they are now governed.

Such are those laws which enact punishments for a very great variety of actions designated crimes; while those from whom such actions proceed, are regularly trained to acquire no other knowledge than that which compels them to conclude, that those actions are the best they could perform.

How much longer shall we continue to allow generation after generation to be taught crime from their infancy, and, when so taught, hunt them like beasts of the forests, until they are entangled beyond escape in the toils and nets of the law? when, if the circumstances of those poor unpitied sufferers had been reversed with those who are even surrounded with the pomp and dignity of justice, these latter would have been at the bar of the culprit, and the former would have been in the judgement seat.

Had the present Judges of these realms been born and educated among the poor and profligate of St. Giles's,[21] or some similar situation, is it not certain, inasmuch as they possess native energies and abilities, that ere this they would have been at the head of their then profession, and, in consequence of that superiority and proficiency, would have already suffered imprisonment, transportation, or death? Can we for a moment hesitate to decide, that, if some of those men whom the laws, dispensed by the present Judges, have doomed to suffer capital punishments, had been born, trained, and circumstanced as these Judges were born, trained, and circumstanced; that some of those who had so suffered, would have been the identical individuals who would have passed the same awful sentences on the present highly esteemed dignitaries of the law?

If we open our eyes and attentively notice events, we shall observe these facts to multiply before us. Is the evil then of so small magnitude as to be totally disregarded and passed by as the ordinary occurrences of the day, and as not deserving of one reflection? And shall we be longer told, 'that the convenient time to attend to inquiries of this nature is not yet come; that other matters of far weightier import engage our attention, and it must remain over till a season of more leisure?'

To those who may be inclined to think and speak thus, I would say, 'Let feelings of humanity or strict justice induce you to devote a few hours to visit some of the public prisons of the metropolis, and patiently inquire, with kind commiserating solicitude, of their various inhabitants, the events of their lives, and the lives of their connections. They will tales unfold that must arrest attention, that will disclose sufferings, misery, and injustice, upon which, for obvious reasons, I will not now dwell, but which, previously, I am persuaded, you could not suppose it possible to exist in any civilized state, far less that they should be permitted for centuries to increase around the very fountain of British jurisprudence.' The true cause however of this conduct, so contrary to the general humanity of the natives of these Islands, is, that a practicable remedy for the evil, on clearly defined and sound principles, had not yet been suggested. But the principles developed in this 'New View of Society' will point out a remedy which is almost simplicity itself, possessing no more practical difficulties than many of the common employments of life; and such as are readily overcome by men of very ordinary practical talents.

That such a remedy is easily practicable, may be collected from the account of the following very partial experiment.

In the year 1784 the late Mr. Dale[22] of Glasgow founded a manufactory for spinning of cotton near the falls of the Clyde, in the county of Lanark in Scotland; and about that period cotton mills were first introduced[23] into the northern part of the kingdom.

It was the power which could be obtained from the falls of water which induced Mr. Dale to erect his mills in this situation, for in other respects it was not well chosen; the country around was uncultivated; the inhabitants were poor, and few in number; and the roads in the neighbourhood were so bad, that the Falls now so celebrated were then unknown to strangers.

It was therefore necessary to collect a new population to supply the infant establishment with labourers. This however was no light task; for all the regularly trained Scotch peasantry disdained the idea of working early and late, day after day, within cotton mills. Two modes then only remained of obtaining these labourers: the one, to procure children from the various public charities of the country; and the other, to induce families to settle around the works.

To accommodate the first, a large house was erected, which ultimately contained about five hundred children, who were procured chiefly from workhouses and charities in Edinburgh. These children were to be fed, clothed, and educated; and these duties Mr. Dale performed with the unwearied benevolence which it is well known he possessed.

To obtain the second, a village was built, and the houses were let at a low rent to such families as could be induced to accept employment in the mills: but such was the general dislike to that occupation at the time, that, with a few exceptions, only persons destitute of friends, employment, and character, were found willing to try the experiment; and of these a sufficient number to supply a constant increase of the manufactory could not be obtained. It was therefore deemed a favour on the part even of such individuals to reside at the village, and when taught the business they grew so valuable to the establishment, that they became agents not to be governed contrary to their own inclinations.

Mr. Dale's principal avocations were at a distance from the works, which he seldom visited more than once for a few hours in three or four months: he was therefore under the necessity of committing the management of the establishment to various servants with more or less power.

Those who have a practical knowledge of mankind will readily anticipate the character which a population so collected and constituted would acquire; it is therefore scarcely necessary to state, that the community by degrees was formed under these circumstances into a very wretched society; every man did that which was right in his own eyes, and vice and immorality prevailed to a monstrous extent. The population lived in idleness, in poverty, in almost every kind of crime; consequently in debt, out of health, and in misery. Yet to make matters still worse,—although the cause proceeded from the best possible motive, a conscientious adherence to principle,—the whole was under a strong sectarian influence, which gave a marked and decided preference to one set of religious opinions over all others, and the professors of the favoured opinions were the privileged of the community.

The boarding-house containing the children presented a very different scene. The benevolent proprietor spared no expense to give comfort to the poor children. The rooms provided for them were spacious, always clean, and well ventilated; the food was abundant, and of the best quality; the clothes were neat and useful; a surgeon was kept in constant pay to direct how to prevent or to cure disease; and the best instructors which the country afforded were appointed to teach such branches of education as were deemed likely to be useful to children in their situation. Kind and well disposed persons were appointed to superintend all their proceedings. Nothing, in short, at first sight seemed wanting to render it a most complete charity.

But to defray the expense of these well devised arrangements, and support the establishment generally, it was absolutely necessary that the children should be employed within the mills from six o'clock in the morning till seven in the evening, summer and winter; and after these hours their education commenced. The directors of the public charities, from mistaken economy, would not consent to send the children under their care to cotton mills, unless the children were received by the proprietors at the ages of six, seven, and eight.[24] And Mr. Dale was under the necessity of accepting them at those ages, or of stopping the manufactory which he had commenced.

It is not to be supposed that children so young could remain, with the interval of meals only, from six in the morning until seven in the evening, in constant employment on their feet within cotton mills, and afterwards acquire much proficiency in education. And so it proved; for many of them became dwarfs in body and mind, and some of them were deformed. Their labour through the day, and their education at night, became so irksome, that numbers of them continually ran away, and almost all looked forward with impatience and anxiety to the expiration of their apprenticeship of seven, eight, and nine years; which generally expired when they were from thirteen to fifteen years old. At this period of life, unaccustomed to provide for themselves, and unacquainted with the world, they usually went to Edinburgh or Glasgow, where boys and girls were soon assailed by the innumerable temptations which all large towns present; and to which many of them fell sacrifices.

Thus Mr. Dale's arrangements and kind solicitude for the comfort and happiness of these children were rendered in their ultimate effect almost nugatory. They were hired by him, and sent to be employed, and without their labour he could not support them; but, while under his care, he did all that any individual, circumstanced as he was, could do for his fellow-creatures. The error proceeded from the children being sent from the workhouses at an age much too young for employment; they ought to have been detained four years longer, and educated; and then some of the evils which followed would have been prevented.

If such be a true picture, not overcharged, of parish apprentices to our manufacturing system, under the best and most humane regulations, in what colours must it be exhibited under the worst?

Mr. Dale was advancing in years; he had no son to succeed him; and finding the consequences just described to be the result of all his strenuous exertions for the improvement and happiness of his fellow-creatures, it is not surprising that he became disposed to retire from the cares of the establishment. He accordingly sold it to some English merchants and manufacturers;[25] one of whom, under the circumstances just narrated, undertook the management of the concern, and fixed his residence in the midst of the population. This individual had been previously in the management of large establishments, employing a number of work-people in the neighbourhood of Manchester; and in every case, by the steady application of certain general principles, he succeeded in reforming the habits of those under his care, and who always among their associates in similar employment appeared conspicuous for their good conduct. With this previous success in remodelling English character, but ignorant of the local ideas, manners, and customs of those now committed to his management, the stranger commenced his task.

At that period the lower classes in Scotland, like those of other countries, had strong prejudices against strangers having any authority over them, and particularly against the English; few of whom had then settled in Scotland, and not one in the neighbourhood of the scenes under description. It is also well known that even the Scotch peasantry and working classes possess the habit of making observations and reasoning thereon with great acuteness; and in the present case, those employed naturally concluded that the new purchasers intended merely to make the utmost profit by the establishment, from the abuses of which many of themselves were then deriving support. The persons employed at these works were therefore strongly prejudiced against the new director of the establishment; prejudiced, because he was a stranger and from England; because he succeeded Mr. Dale, under whose proprietorship they acted almost as they liked; because his religious creed was not theirs; and because they concluded that the works would be governed by new laws and regulations, calculated to squeeze, as they often termed it, the greatest gain out of their labour.

In consequence, from the day he arrived among them, every means which ingenuity could devise was set to work to counteract the plan which he attempted to introduce; and for two years it was a regular attack and defence of prejudices and mal-practices between the manager and population of the place; without the former being able to make much progress, or convince the latter of the sincerity of his good intentions for their welfare. He however did not lose his patience, his temper, or his confidence in the certain success of the principles on which he founded his conduct. These principles ultimately prevailed: the population could not continue to resist a firm well-directed kindness administering justice to all. They therefore slowly and cautiously began to give him some portion of their confidence; and, as this increased, he was enabled more and more to develop his plans for their amelioration. It may with truth be said, that at this period they possessed almost all the vices and very few of the virtues of a social community. Theft and the receipt of stolen goods was their trade, idleness and drunkenness their habit, falsehood and deception their garb, dissentions civil and religious their daily practice: they united only in a zealous systematic opposition to their employers.

Here, then, was a fair field on which to try the efficacy in practice of principles supposed capable of altering any characters. The manager formed his plans accordingly: he spent some time in finding out the full extent of the evil against which he had to contend, and in tracing the true causes which had produced, and were continuing, those effects. He found that all was distrust, disorder, and disunion; and he wished to introduce confidence, regularity, and harmony: he therefore began to bring forward his various expedients to withdraw the unfavourable circumstances by which they had been hitherto surrounded, and replace them by others calculated to produce a more happy result. He soon discovered that theft was extended through almost all the ramifications of the community, and the receipt of stolen goods through all the country around. To remedy this evil, not one legal punishment was inflicted, not one individual imprisoned, even for an hour: but checks and other regulations of prevention were introduced; a short plain explanation of the immediate benefits they would derive from a different conduct was inculcated by those instructed for the purpose, who had the best powers of reasoning among themselves. They were at the same time instructed how to direct their industry in legal and useful occupations; by which, without danger or disgrace, they could really earn more than they had previously obtained by dishonest practices.—Thus, the difficulty of committing the crime was increased, the detection afterwards rendered more easy, the habit of honest industry formed, and the pleasure of good conduct experienced.

Drunkenness was attacked in the same manner: it was discountenanced on every occasion by those who had charge of any department: its destructive and pernicious effects were frequently stated by his own more prudent comrades, at the proper moment, when the individual was soberly suffering from the effects of his previous excess: pot- and public-houses were gradually removed from the immediate vicinity of their dwellings: the health and comfort of temperance were made familiar to them: by degrees drunkenness disappeared, and many who were habitual bacchanalians are now conspicuous for undeviating sobriety.

Falsehood and deception met with a similar fate; they were held in disgrace, their practical evils were shortly explained; and every countenance was given to truth and open conduct. The pleasure and substantial advantages derived from the latter, soon overcame the impolicy, error, and consequent misery which the former mode of acting had created.

Dissentions and quarrels were undermined by analogous expedients. When they could not be readily adjusted between the parties themselves, they were stated to the manager; and as in such cases both disputants were usually more or less in the wrong, that wrong was in as few words as possible explained, forgiveness and friendship recommended, and one simple and easily remembered precept inculcated, as the most valuable rule for their whole conduct, and the advantages of which they would experience every moment of their lives:—viz. 'That in future they should endeavour to use the same active exertions to make each other happy and comfortable, as they had hitherto done to make each other miserable; and, by carrying this short memorandum in their mind, and applying it on all occasions, they would soon render that place a paradise, which, from the most mistaken principles of action, they now made the abode of misery.'—The experiment was tried, the parties enjoyed the gratification of this new mode of conduct; references rapidly subsided, and now serious differences are scarcely known.

Considerable jealousies also existed on account of one religious sect possessing a decided preference over the others. This was corrected by discontinuing that preference, and giving an uniform encouragement to those who conducted themselves well, among all the various religious persuasions; by recommending the same consideration to be shown to the conscientious opinions of each sect, on the ground that all must believe the particular doctrines which they had been taught, and consequently all were in that respect upon an equal footing; nor was it possible yet to say which was right, or which wrong. It was likewise inculcated, that all should attend to the essence of religion, and not act as the world was now taught and trained to do: that is, to overlook the substance and essence of religion, and devote their talents, time, and money, to that which is far worse than its shadow, sectarianism; another term for something very injurious to society, and very absurd, which one or other well meaning enthusiast has added to true religion; which, without these defects, would soon form those characters which every wise and good man is anxious to see.

Such statements and conduct arrested sectarian animosity and ignorant intolerance; each retains full liberty of conscience, and in consequence each partakes of the sincere friendship of many sects instead of one. They act with cordiality together in the same departments and pursuits, and associate as though the whole community were not of different sectarian persuasions: and not one evil ensues.

The same principles were applied to correct the irregular intercourse of the sexes;—such conduct was discountenanced and held in disgrace; fines were levied upon both parties for the use of the support fund[26] of the community. But because they had once unfortunately offended against the established laws and customs of society, they were not forced to become vicious, abandoned, and miserable. The door was left open for them to return to the comforts of kind friends and respected acquaintance; and, beyond any previous expectation, the evil became greatly diminished.

The system of receiving apprentices[27] from public charities was abolished; permanent settlers with large families were encouraged, and comfortable houses were built for their accommodation.

The practice of employing children in the mills, of six, seven, and eight years of age, was discontinued, and their parents advised to allow them to acquire health and education until they were ten years old.[28]

The children were taught reading, writing, and arithmetic, during five years, that is, from five to ten, in the village school, without expense to their parents. All the modern improvements in education have been adopted, or are in process of adoption.[29] They may therefore be taught and well trained before they engage in any regular employment. Another important consideration is, that all their instruction is rendered a pleasure and delight to them; they are much more anxious for the hour of school time to arrive than to end: they therefore make a rapid progress; and it may be safely asserted, that if they shall not be trained to form such characters as may be the most desired, the fault will not proceed from the children; the cause will be in the want of a true knowledge of human nature in those who have the management of them and their parents.

During the period that these changes were going forward, attention was given to the domestic arrangements of the community. Their houses were rendered more comfortable, their streets were improved, the best provisions were purchased, and sold to them at low rates, yet covering the original expense;[30] and under such regulations as taught them how to proportion their expenditure to their income. Fuel and clothes were obtained for them in the same manner; and no advantage was ever attempted to be taken of them, or means used to deceive them.

In consequence, their animosity and opposition to the stranger subsided, their full confidence was obtained, and they became satisfied that no evil was intended them: they were convinced that a real desire existed to increase their happiness, upon those grounds alone on which it could be permanently increased. All difficulties in the way of future improvement vanished. They were taught to be rational, and they acted rationally; thus both parties experienced the incalculable advantages of the system which had been adopted. Those employed became industrious, temperate, healthy; faithful to their employers, and kind to each other; while the proprietors were deriving services from their attachment, almost without inspection, far beyond those which could be obtained by any other means than those of mutual confidence and kindness. Such was the effect of these principles on the adults; on those whose previous habits had been as ill formed as habits could be; and certainly the application of the principles to practice was made under the most unfavourable circumstances.

These principles, applied to the community at New Lanark, at first under many of the most discouraging circumstances, but persevered in for sixteen years, effected a complete change in the general character of the village, containing upwards of two thousand inhabitants, and into which, also, there was a constant influx of new comers.—But as the promulgation of new miracles is not for present times, it is not pretended that under such circumstances one and all are become wise and good; or, that they are free from error: but it may be truly stated, that they now constitute a very improved society, that their worst habits are gone, and that their minor ones will soon disappear under a continuance of the application of the same principles; that during the period mentioned, scarcely a legal punishment has been inflicted, or an application been made for parish funds by any individual among them. Drunkenness is not seen in their streets, and the children are taught and trained in the institution for forming their character without any punishment. The community exhibits the general appearance of industry, temperance, comfort, health, and happiness.—These are and ever will be the sure and certain effects of the adoption of the principles explained; and these principles, applied with judgement, will effectually reform the most vicious community existing, and train the younger part of it to any character which may be desired; and that, too, much more easily on an extended than on a limited scale.—To apply these principles, however, successfully to practice, both a comprehensive and a minute view must be taken of the existing state of the society on which they are intended to operate. The causes of the most prevalent evils must be accurately traced, and those means which appear the most easy and simple should be immediately applied to remove them.

In this progress the smallest alteration, adequate to produce any good effect, should be made at one time; indeed, if possible, the change should be so gradual as to be almost imperceptible, yet always making a permanent advance in the desired improvements. By this procedure, the most rapid practical progress will be obtained, because the inclination to resistance will be removed, and time will be given for reason to weaken the force of long established injurious prejudices. The removal of the first evil will prepare the way for the removal of the second; and this facility will increase, not in an arithmetical, but in a geometrical proportion; until the directors of the system will themselves be gratified beyond expression with the beneficial magnitude of their own proceedings.

Nor while these principles shall be acted upon can there be any retrogression in this good work; for the permanence of the amelioration will be equal to its extent.

What then remains to prevent such a system from being immediately adopted into national practice? Nothing, surely, but a general distribution of the knowledge of the practice. For, with the certain means of preventing crimes, can it be supposed that British legislators, as soon as these means shall be made evident, will longer withhold them from their fellow subjects? No: I am persuaded that neither prince, ministers, parliament, nor any party in church or state, will avow inclination to act on principles of such flagrant injustice.[31] Have they not on many occasions evinced a sincere and ardent desire to ameliorate the condition of the subjects of the empire, when practicable means of amelioration were explained to them, which could be adopted without risking the safety of the state? They have, it is true, refused one measure called a reform,[32] and most wise have they been in persevering in that refusal. But the advocates for that measure, well-intentioned and patriotic as many of them are, cannot show any good practical effects to be derived from it in the present state of ignorance in which the mass of the British population has been hitherto allowed to be trained. On the contrary, no rational being can attentively observe the scenes exhibited during every general election, and wish for those scenes to be extended. That, indeed, would be to wish any thing but a reform of the manners, habits and principles of our abused and deluded fellow subjects.

Away then with this abuse of terms! It would not, and while the present circumstances continue, it could not be reform; but, if now adopted, it would soon terminate in anarchy and confusion.

For some time to come there can be but one practicable, and therefore one rational reform, which without danger can be attempted in these realms; a reform in which all men and all parties may join—that is, a reform in the training and in the management of the poor, the ignorant, the untaught and untrained, or ill taught and ill trained, among the whole mass of British population; and a plain, simple, practicable plan, which would not contain the least danger to any individual, or to any part of society, may be devised for that purpose.

That plan is a national, well digested, unexclusive system for the formation of character, and general amelioration of the lower orders.

Train any population rationally, and they will be rational. Furnish honest and useful employments to those so trained, and such employments they will greatly prefer to dishonest or injurious occupations. It is beyond all calculation the interest of every government to provide that training and that employment: and to provide both is easily practicable.

The first, as before stated, is to be obtained by a national system for the formation of character; the second, by governments preparing a reserve of employment for the surplus working classes, when the general demand for labour throughout the country is not equal to the full occupation of the whole: that employment to be on useful national objects, from which the public may derive advantage equal to the expense which those works may require.

The national plan for the formation of character should include all the modern improvements of education, without regard to the system of any one individual; and should not exclude the child of any one subject in the empire. Any thing short of this would be an act of intolerance and injustice to the excluded, and of injury to society, so glaring and manifest, that I shall be deceived in the character of my countrymen, if any of those who have influence in church or state should now be found willing to attempt it. Is it not indeed strikingly evident even to common observers, that any further effort to enforce religious exclusion would involve the certain and speedy destruction of the present church establishment, and would even endanger our civil institutions?

99

It may be said, however, that ministers and parliament have many other important subjects under discussion. This is evidently true; but will they not have high national concerns always to engage their attention? And can any question be brought forward of deeper interest to the community than that which affects the formation of character and the well-being of every individual within the empire? a question too which, when understood, will be found to offer the means of amelioration to the revenues of these kingdoms, far beyond any practical plan now likely to be devised. Yet, important as are considerations of revenue, they must appear secondary when put in competition with the lives, liberty, and comfort of our fellow subjects.

## ESSAY THIRD

### The Principles of the Former Essays applied to a Particular Situation

At the conclusion of the Second Essay, a promise was made that an account should be given of the plans which were in progress at New Lanark for the further improvement of its inhabitants; and that a practical system should be sketched, by which equal advantages might be generally introduced among the poor and working classes throughout the United Kingdom.

This account became necessary, in order to exhibit even a limited view of the principles on which the plans of the author are founded, and to recommend them generally to practice.

That which has been hitherto done for the community of New Lanark, as described in the Second Essay, has chiefly consisted in withdrawing some of those circumstances which tended to generate, continue, or increase early bad habits; that is to say, undoing that which society had from ignorance permitted to be done.

To effect this, however, was a far more difficult task than to train up a child[33] from infancy in the way he should go, for that is the most easy process for the formation of character; while to unlearn and to change long acquired habits, is a proceeding directly opposed to the most tenacious feelings of human nature.

Nevertheless the proper application steadily pursued did effect beneficial changes on these old habits, even beyond the most sanguine expectations of the party by whom the task was undertaken. The principles were derived from the study of human nature itself, and they could not fail of success.

Still, however, very little, comparatively speaking, had been done for them. They had not been taught the most valuable domestic and social habits: such as the most economical method of preparing food; how to arrange their dwellings with neatness, and to keep them always clean and in order; but what was of infinitely more importance, they had not been instructed how to train their children, to form them into valuable members of the community, or to know that principles existed, which, when properly applied to practice from infancy, would insure from man to man, without chance of failure, a just, open, sincere and benevolent conduct.

It was in this stage of the progress of improvement, that it became necessary to form arrangements for surrounding them with circumstances, which should gradually prepare the individuals to receive and firmly retain those domestic and social acquirements and habits.

For this purpose a building which may be termed the 'New Institution',[34] was erected in the centre of the establishment, with an inclosed area before it. The area is intended for a playground for the children of the villagers, from the time they can walk alone until they enter the school.

It must be evident to those who have been in the practice of observing children with attention, that much of good or evil is taught to or acquired by a child at a very early period of its life; that much of temper or disposition is correctly or incorrectly formed before he attains his second year; and that many durable impressions are made at the termination of the first twelve or even six months of his existence. The children therefore of the uninstructed and ill-instructed suffer material injury in the formation of their characters, during these and the subsequent years of childhood and of youth.

It was to prevent, or as much as possible to counteract, these primary evils, to which the poor and working classes are exposed when infants, that the area became part of the New Institution.

Into this play-ground the children are to be received as soon as they can freely walk alone; to be superintended by persons instructed to take charge of them.

As the happiness of man chiefly, if not altogether, depends on his own sentiments and habits, as well as those of the individuals around him; and as any sentiments and habits may be given to all infants, it becomes of primary importance that those alone should be given to them which can contribute to their happiness. Each child therefore, on his entrance into the play-ground, is to be told in language which he can understand, that 'he is never to injure his playfellows, but on the contrary he is to contribute all in his power to make them happy'. This simple precept, when comprehended in all its bearings, and the habits which will arise from its early adoption into practice, if no counteracting principles shall be forced on the young mind, will effectually supersede all the errors which have hitherto kept the world in ignorance and misery. So simple a precept, too, will be easily taught, and as easily acquired; for the chief employment of the superintendants will be to prevent any deviation from it in practice. The older children, when they shall have experienced the endless advantages from acting on this principle, will, by their example, soon enforce the practice of it on the young strangers; and the happiness which the little groups will enjoy from this rational conduct, will insure its speedy and general and willing adoption. The habit also which they will acquire at this early period of life, by continually acting on the principle, will fix it firmly; it will become easy and familiar to them, or, as it is often termed, natural.

The character thus early formed will be as durable as it will be advantageous to the individual and to the community. This part of the arrangement therefore will effect the following purposes:

The child will be removed,[35] so far as is at present practicable, from the erroneous treatment of the yet untrained and untaught parents.

The parents will be relieved from the loss of time, and from the care and anxiety which are now occasioned by attendance on their children from the period when they can go alone to that at which they enter the school.

The child will be placed in a situation of safety, where, with its future schoolfellows and companions, it will acquire the best habits and principles, while at meal times and at night it will return to the caresses of its parents; and the affections of each are likely to be increased by the separation.

The area[36] is also to be a place of meeting for the children from five to ten years of age, previous to and after school-hours, and to serve for a drill ground, the object of which will be hereafter explained. And a shade will be formed, under which, in stormy weather, the children may retire for shelter.

These are the important purposes to which a play-ground attached to a school may be applied.

Those who have derived a knowledge of human nature from observation know, that man in every situation requires relaxation from his constant and regular occupations, whatever they may be; and that, if he shall not be provided with or permitted to enjoy innocent and uninjurious amusements, he must and will partake of those which he can obtain, to give him temporary relief from his exertions, although the means of gaining that relief should be most pernicious. For man, irrationally instructed, is ever influenced far more by immediate feelings than by remote considerations.

Those, then, who desire to give mankind the character which it would be for the happiness of all that they should possess, will not fail to make careful provision for their amusement and recreation.

The Sabbath[37] was originally so intended. It was instituted to be a day of universal enjoyment and happiness to the human race. It is frequently made, however, from the opposite extremes of error, either a day of superstitious gloom and tyranny over the mind, or of the most destructive intemperance and licentiousness. The Sabbath, in many parts of Scotland, is not now a day of innocent and cheerful recreation to the labouring man; nor can those who are confined all the week to sedentary occupations freely partake, without censure, of the air and exercise to which nature invites them, and which their health demands.

The errors of the times of superstition and bigotry still hold some sway, and compel those who wish to preserve a regard to their respectability in society to an overstrained demeanour; and this demeanour sometimes degenerates into hypocrisy, and is often the cause of great inconsistency. It is destructive of every open, honest, generous, and manly feeling. It disgusts many, and drives them to the opposite extreme. It is sometimes the cause of insanity. It is founded in ignorance, and defeats its own object.

While erroneous customs prevail in any country, it would evince an ignorance of human nature in any individual to offend against them, until he has convinced the community of their error.

To counteract, in some degree, the inconvenience which arose from this misapplication of the Sabbath, it became necessary to introduce on the other days of the week some innocent amusement and recreation for those whose labours were unceasing, and in winter almost uniform. In summer, the inhabitants of the village of New Lanark have their gardens and potato-grounds to cultivate; they have walks laid out to give them health, and the habit of being gratified with the ever-changing scenes of nature; for those scenes afford not only the most economical but also the most innocent pleasures which man can enjoy; and all men may be easily trained to enjoy them.

In winter, the community are deprived of these healthy occupations and amusements; they are employed ten hours and three quarters[38] every day in the week, except Sunday, and generally every individual continues during that time at the same work; and experience has shown that the average health and spirits of the community are several degrees lower in winter than in summer, and this in part may be fairly attributed to that cause.

These considerations suggested the necessity of rooms for innocent amusements and rational recreation.

Many well-intentioned individuals, unaccustomed to witness the conduct of those among the lower orders who have been rationally treated and trained, may fancy such an assemblage will necessarily become a scene of confusion and disorder: instead of which, however, it proceeds with uniform propriety; it is highly favourable to the health, spirits, and dispositions of the individuals so engaged; and if any irregularity should arise, the cause will be solely owing to the parties who attempt to direct the proceedings, being deficient in a practical knowledge of human nature.

It has been and ever will be found far more easy to lead mankind to virtue, or to rational conduct, by providing them with well-regulated innocent amusements and recreations, than by forcing them to submit to useless restraints, which tend only to create disgust, and often to connect such feelings even with that which is excellent in itself, merely because it has been injudiciously associated.

Hitherto indeed, in all ages, and in all countries, man seems to have blindly conspired against the happiness of man, and to have remained as ignorant of himself as he was of the solar system prior to the days of Copernicus and Galileo.

Many of the learned and wise among our ancestors were conscious of this ignorance, and deeply lamented its effects; and some of them recommended the partial adoption of those principles which can alone relieve the world from the miserable effects of ignorance.

The time, however, for the emancipation of the human mind was not then arrived, the world was not prepared to receive it. The history of humanity shows it to be an undeviating law of nature, that man shall not prematurely break the shell of ignorance; that he must patiently wait until the principle of knowledge has pervaded the whole mass of the interior, to give it life and strength sufficient to bear the light of day.

Those who have duly reflected on the nature and extent of the mental movements of the world for the last half century, must be conscious that great changes are in progress; that man is about to advance another important step towards that degree of intelligence which his natural powers seem capable of attaining. Observe the transactions of the passing hours; see the whole mass of mind in full motion; behold it momentarily increasing in vigour, and preparing ere long to burst its confinement. But what is to be the nature of this change? A due attention to the facts around us, and to those transmitted by the invention of printing from former ages, will afford a satisfactory reply.

From the earliest ages it has been the practice of the world, to act on the supposition that each individual man forms his own character, and that therefore he is accountable for all his sentiments and habits, and consequently merits reward for some, and punishment for others. Every system which has been established among men has been founded on these erroneous principles. When, however, they shall be brought to the test of fair examination, they will be found not only unsupported, but in direct opposition to all experience, and to the evidence of our senses. This is not a slight mistake which involves only trivial consequences; it is a fundamental error of the highest possible magnitude.

Is it then wisdom to think and to act in opposition to the facts which hourly exhibit themselves around us, and in direct contradiction to the evidence of our senses? Inquire of the most learned and wise of the present day, ask them to speak with sincerity, and they will tell you that they have long known the principles on which society has been founded to be false. Hitherto, however, the tide of public opinion in all countries has been directed by a combination of prejudice, bigotry, and fanaticism, derived from the wildest imaginations of ignorance; and the most enlightened men have not dared to expose those errors which to them were offensive, prominent and glaring.

Happily for man, this reign of ignorance rapidly approaches to dissolution; its terrors are already on the wing, and soon they will be compelled to take their flight, never more to return. For now the knowledge of the existing errors is not only possessed by the learned and reflecting, but it is spreading far and wide throughout society; and ere long it will be fully comprehended even by the most ignorant.

Attempts may indeed be made by individuals, who through ignorance mistake their real interests, to retard the progress of this knowledge; but as it will prove itself to be in unison with the evidence of our senses, and therefore true beyond the possibility of disproof, it cannot be impeded, and in its course will overwhelm all opposition.

It is then by the full and complete disclosure of these principles, that the destruction of ignorance and misery is to be effected, and the reign of reason, intelligence, and happiness, is to be firmly established.

It was necessary to give this development of the principles advocated, that the remaining parts of the New Institution, yet to be described, may be clearly understood. We now proceed to explain the several purposes intended to be accomplished by the School, Lecture-room, and Church.

It must be evident to those who have any powers of reason yet undestroyed, that man is now taught and trained in a theory and practice directly opposed to each other. Hence the perpetual inconsistencies, follies and absurdities, which every one can readily discover in his neighbour, without being conscious that he also possesses similar incongruities. The instruction to be given in the School, Lecture-Room, and Church, is intended to counteract and remedy the evil; and to prove the incalculable advantages which society would derive from the introduction of a theory and practice consistent with each other. The uppermost story of the New Institution is arranged to serve for a School, Lecture-room, and Church. And these are intended to have a direct influence in forming the character of the villagers.

It is comparatively of little avail to give to either young or old 'precept upon precept, and line upon line', except the means shall be also prepared to train them in good practical habits. Hence an education for the untaught and ill-taught becomes of the first importance to the welfare of society: and it is this which has influenced all the arrangements connected with the New Institution.

The time the children will remain under the discipline of the play-ground and school will afford all the opportunity that can be desired, to create, cultivate, and establish those habits and sentiments which tend to the welfare of the individual and of the community. And in conformity to this plan of proceeding, the precept which was given to the child of two years old, on coming into the play-ground, 'that he must endeavour to make his companions happy', is to be renewed and enforced on his entrance into the school; and the first duty of the Schoolmaster will be train his pupils to acquire the practice of always acting on this principle. It is a simple rule, the plain and obvious reasons for which, children at an early age may be readily taught to comprehend: as they advance in years, become familiarised with its practice, and experience the beneficial effects to themselves, they will better feel and understand all its important consequences to society.

Such then being the foundation on which the practical habits of the children are to be formed, we proceed to explain the superstructure.

In addition to the knowledge of the principle and practice of the abovementioned precept, the boys and girls are to be taught in the school to read well, and to understand what they read; to write expeditiously a good legible hand; and to learn correctly, so that they may comprehend, and use with facility, the fundamental rules of arithmetic. The girls are also to be taught to sew, cut out and make up useful family garments; and after acquiring a sufficient knowledge of these, they are to attend in rotation in the public kitchen and eating-rooms; to learn to prepare wholesome food in an economical manner, and to keep a house neat and well arranged.

It was said that the children are to be taught to read well, and to understand what they read.

In many schools, the children of the poor and labouring classes are never taught to understand what they read; the time therefore which is occupied in the mockery of instruction is lost; in other schools, the children, through the ignorance of their instructors, are taught to believe without reasoning, and thus never to think or to reason correctly. These truly lamentable practices cannot fail to indispose the young mind for plain, simple, and rational instruction.

The books by which it is now the common custom to teach children to read, inform them of any thing except that which, at their age, they ought to be taught: hence the inconsistencies and follies of adults. It is full time that this system should be changed. Can man, when possessing the full vigour of his faculties, form a rational judgement on any subject, until he has first collected all the facts respecting it, which are known? Has not this ever been, and will not this ever remain, the only path by which human knowledge can be obtained? Then children ought to be instructed on the same principles. They should first be taught the knowledge of facts,[39] commencing with those which are the most familiar to the young mind, and gradually proceeding to the most useful and necessary to be known by the respective individuals in the rank of life in which they are likely to be placed; and in all cases the children should have as clear an explanation of each fact as their minds can comprehend, rendering those explanations more detailed as the child acquires strength and capacity of intellect.

As soon as the young mind shall be duly prepared for such instruction, the master should not allow any opportunity to escape, that would enable him to enforce the clear and inseparable connection which exists between the interest and happiness of each individual, and the interest and happiness of every other individual. This should be the beginning and end of all his instruction:

and by degrees it will be so well understood by his pupils, that they will receive the same conviction of its truth, that those familiar with mathematics now entertain of the demonstrations of Euclid. And when thus comprehended, the all-prevailing principle of known life, the desire of happiness, will compel them without deviation to pursue it in practice.

It is much to be regretted that the strength and capacity of the minds of children are yet unknown:[40] their faculties have been hitherto estimated by the folly of the instruction which has been given to them; while, if they were never taught to acquire error, they would speedily exhibit such powers of mind, as would convince the most incredulous how much human intellect has been injured by the ignorance of former and present treatment.

It is therefore indeed important that the mind from its birth should receive those ideas only, which are consistent with each other, which are in unison with all the known facts of the creation, and which are therefore true.

Let the plan which has now been recommended, be steadily put in practice from infancy, without counteraction from the systems of education which now exist; and characters even in youth may be formed, that in true knowledge, and in every good and valuable quality, will not only greatly surpass the wise and learned of the present and preceding times, but appear, as they really will be, a race of rational, or superior beings. It is true, this change cannot be instantaneously established; it cannot be created by magic, or by a miracle; it must be effected gradually—and to accomplish it finally, will prove a work of labour and of years. For those who have been misinstructed from infancy, who have now influence, and are active in the world, and whose activity is directed by the false notions of their fore-fathers, will of course endeavour to obstruct the change. Those who have been systematically impressed with early errors, and conscientiously think them to be truths, will of necessity, while such errors remain, en-deavour to perpetuate them in their children. Some simple but general method, therefore, becomes neces-sary to counteract as speedily as possible an evil of so formidable a magnitude.

It was this view of the subject which suggested the utility of preparing the means to admit of evening lectures[41] in the New Institution; and it is intended they should be given, during winter, three nights in the week, alternately with dancing.

To the ill-trained and ill-taught these lectures may be made invaluable; and these are now numerous; for the far greater part of the population of the world has been permitted to pass the proper season of instruction without being trained to be rational; and they have acquired only the ideas and habits which proceed from ignorant association and erroneous instruction.

It is intended that the lectures should be familiar discourses, delivered in plain impressive language, to instruct the adult part of the community in the most useful practical parts of knowledge in which they are deficient, particularly in the proper method of training their children to become rational creatures; how to expend the earnings of their own labour to advantage; and how to appropriate the surplus gains which will be left to them, in order to create a fund which will relieve them from the anxious fear of future want, and thus give them, under the many errors of the present sys-tems, that rational confidence in their own exertions and good conduct, without which, consistency of character or domestic comfort cannot be obtained, and ought not to be expected. The young people may be also questioned relative to their progress in useful knowledge, and allowed to ask for explanations. In short, these lectures may be made to convey, in an amusing and agreeable manner, highly valuable and substantial information to those who are now the most ignorant in the community; and by similar means, which at a trifling expense may be put into action over the whole kingdom, the most important benefits may be given to the labouring classes, and, through them, to the whole mass of society.

For it should be considered, that the far greater part of the population belong to or have risen from the labouring classes; and by them the happiness and comfort of all ranks, not excluding the highest, are very essentially influenced; because even much more of the character of children in all families is formed by the servants, than is ever supposed by those unaccustomed to trace with attention the human mind from earliest infancy. It is indeed impossible that children in any situation can be correctly trained, until those who surround them from infancy shall be previously well instructed: and the value of good servants may be duly appreciated by those who have experienced the difference between the very good and very bad.

The last part of the intended arrangement of the New Institution remains yet to be described. This is the church and its doctrines; and they involve considerations of the highest interest and importance; inasmuch as a knowledge of truth on the subject of religion would permanently establish the happiness of man; for it is the inconsistencies alone, proceeding from the want of this knowledge, which have created, and still create, a great proportion of the miseries which exist in the world.

The only certain criterion of truth is, that it is ever consistent with itself; it remains one and the same, under every view and comparison of it which can be made; while error will not stand the test of this investigation and comparison, because it ever leads to absurd conclusions.

Had any one of the various opposing systems which have governed the world, and disunited man from man, been true, without any mixture of error,—that system, very speedily after its public promulgation, would have pervaded society, and compelled all men to have acknowledged its truth.

The criterion however which has been stated shows that they are all, without an exception, in part inconsistent with the facts which exist around us. Those systems therefore must have contained some fundamental errors; and it is utterly impossible for man to become rational, or enjoy the happiness which he is capable of attaining, until those errors are exposed and annihilated.

The doctrines which have been and now are taught throughout the world must necessarily create and perpetuate, and they do create and perpetuate, a total want of mental charity among men. They also generate superstition, bigotry, hypocrisy, hatred, revenge, wars, and all their evil consequences. For it has been and is a fundamental principle in every system hitherto taught, with exceptions more nominal than real, 'That man will possess merit, and receive eternal reward, by believing the doctrines of that peculiar system; that he will be eternally punished if he disbelieves them; that all those innumerable individuals also, who, through time, have not been taught to believe other than the tenets of this system, must be doomed to eternal misery.' Yet nature itself, in all its works, is perpetually operating to convince man of such gross absurdities.

Yes, my deluded fellow-men, believe me, for your future happiness, that the facts around us, when you shall observe them aright, will make it evident even to demonstration, that all such doctrines must be erroneous, because the will of man has no power whatever over his opinions; he must, and ever did, and ever will, believe what has been, is, or may be impressed on his mind by his predecessors, and the circumstances which surround him.

It is from these fundamental errors in all systems which have been hitherto taught to the mass of mankind, that the misery of the human race has to so great an extent proceeded; for, in consequence of it, man has been always instructed from infancy to believe impossibilities; he is still taught to pursue the same insane course, and the result still is misery. Let this source of wretchedness, this most lamentable of all errors, this scourge of the human race, be publicly exposed; and let those just principles be introduced, which prove themselves true by their uniform consistency and the evidence of our senses: hence insincerity, hatred, revenge, and even a wish to injure a fellow-creature, will ere long be unknown; and mental charity, heartfelt benevolence, and acts of kindness to one another, will be the distinguishing characteristics of human nature.

Difficult as it may be to establish this grand truth generally throughout society, on account of the dark and gross errors in which the world to this period has been instructed, it will be found, whenever the subject shall undergo a full investigation, that the principles now brought forward cannot, by possibility, injure any class of men, or even a single individual.

The principle then on which the doctrines taught in the New Institution are proposed to be founded, is, that they shall be in unison with universally revealed facts which cannot but be true.

The following are some of the facts which, with a view to this part of the undertaking, may be deemed fundamental.

That man is born with a desire to obtain happiness, which desire is the primary cause of all his actions, continues through life, and, in popular language, is called self-interest.[42]

That the desire of happiness in man, the germs of his natural inclinations, and the faculties by which he acquires knowledge, are formed, unknown to himself, in the womb; and, whether perfect or imperfect, they are alone the immediate work of the Creator, and over which the infant and future man have no control.

That these inclinations and faculties are not formed exactly alike in any two individuals: hence the diversity of talents, and the varied impressions called liking, and disliking, which the same external objects make on different persons, and the lesser varieties which exist among men whose characters have been formed apparently under similar circumstances.

That the knowledge which man receives, is derived from the objects around him, and chiefly from the example and instruction of his immediate predecessors.

That when the knowledge which he receives is true, and unmixed with error, although it be limited, if the community in which he lives possesses the same kind and degree of knowledge, he will enjoy happiness in proportion to the extent of that knowledge. On the contrary, when the opinions which he receives are erroneous, and the opinions possessed by the community in which he resides are equally erroneous, his misery will be in proportion to the extent of those erroneous opinions.

That when the knowledge which man receives shall be extended to its utmost limit, and true without any mixture of error, then he may and will enjoy all the happiness of which his nature will be capable.

That it consequently becomes of the first and highest importance that man should be taught to distinguish truth from error.

That man has no other means of discovering what is false, except by his faculty of reason, or power of acquiring and comparing the ideas which he receives.

That all men are erroneously trained at present, and hence the inconsistences and misery of the world.

That the fundamental errors now impressed from infancy on the minds of all men, and from whence all their other errors proceed, are, that they form their own individual characters, and possess merit or demerit for the peculiar notions impressed on the mind during its early growth.

That the evil and misery which arise from accidents, disease, and death, are also greatly increased and extended by man's ignorance of himself.

That when these truths are made evident, every individual will necessarily endeavour to promote the happiness of every other individual within his sphere of action; because he must clearly, and without any doubt, comprehend such conduct to be the essence of self-interest, or the true cause of self-happiness.

Here then is a firm foundation on which to erect

vital religion, pure and undefiled, and the only one which, without any counteracting evil, can give peace and happiness to man.

It is to bring into practical operation, in forming the characters of men, these most important of all truths, that the religious part of the Institution at New Lanark will be chiefly directed; and such are the fundamental principles upon which the Instructor will proceed.

They are thus publicly avowed before all men, that they may undergo discussion, and the most severe scrutiny and investigation.

Having alluded to the chief uses of the playground and exercise-rooms, with the School, Lecture-room, and Church, it remains, to complete the account of the New Institution, that the object of the drill exercise,[43] mentioned when stating the purposes of the playground, should be explained; and to this we proceed.

Were all men trained to be rational, the art of war would be rendered useless. While, however, any part of mankind shall be taught that they form their own characters, and continue to be trained from infancy to think and act irrationally; that is, to acquire feelings of enmity, and to deem it a duty to engage in war, against those who have been instructed to differ from them in sentiments and habits; even the most rational must, for their personal security, learn the means of defence; and every community of such characters, while surrounded by men who have been thus improperly taught, should acquire a knowledge of this destructive art, that they may be enabled to overrule the actions of irrational beings, and maintain peace.

To accomplish these objects to the utmost practical limit, and with the least inconvenience, every male should be instructed how best to defend, when attacked, the community to which he belongs. And these advantages are only to be obtained by providing proper means for the instruction of all boys in the use of arms and the arts of war.

As an example how easily and effectually this might be accomplished over the British Isles, it is intended that the boys trained and educated in the Institution at New Lanark shall be thus instructed; that the person appointed to attend the children in the play-ground shall be qualified to drill and teach the boys the manual exercise, and that he shall be frequently so employed. That afterwards fire-arms, of proportionate weight and size to the age and strength of the boys, shall be provided for them; when also they might be taught to practise and understand the more complicated military movements.

This exercise, properly administered, will greatly contribute to the health and spirits of the boys, give them an erect and proper form, and habits of attention, celerity, and order. They will however be taught to consider this exercise an art rendered absolutely necessary by the partial insanity of some of their fellow-creatures, who, by the errors of their predecessors transmitted through preceding generations, have been taught to acquire feelings of enmity increasing to madness against those who could not avoid differing from them in sentiments and habits; that this art should never be brought into practice except to restrain the violence of such madmen; and in these cases it should be administered with the least possible severity; and solely to prevent the evil consequences of those rash actions of the insane, and if possible cure them of their disease.

Thus, in a few years, by foresight and arrangement, may almost the whole expense and inconvenience attending the local military be superseded, and a permanent force created, which in numbers, discipline, and principles, would be superior beyond all comparison for the purposes of defence, always ready in case of need, yet without the loss which is now sustained by the community of efficient and valuable labour. The expenditure which would be saved by this simple expedient would be far more than competent to educate the whole of the poor and labouring classes of these kingdoms.

There is still another arrangement in contemplation for the community at New Lanark, and without which the establishment will remain incomplete.

It is an expedient to enable the individuals, by their own foresight, prudence, and industry, to secure to themselves in old age a comfortable provision and asylum.

Those now employed at the establishment contribute to a fund which supports them when too ill to work, or when superannuated. This fund, however, is not calculated to give them more than a bare existence; and it is surely desirable that, after they have spent nearly half a century in unremitting industry, they should, if possible, in the decline of life, enjoy a comfortable independence.

To effect this object, it is intended that in the most pleasant situation near the present village, neat and convenient dwellings should be erected, with gardens attached; that they should be surrounded and sheltered by plantations, through which public walks should be formed, and the whole arranged to give the occupiers the most substantial comforts.

That these dwellings, with the privileges of the public walks, &c. shall become the property of those individuals who, without compulsion, shall subscribe such equitable sums monthly as, in a given number of years, will be equal to their purchase, and to a create a fund from which, when these individuals become occupiers of their new residences, they may receive weekly, monthly, or quarterly payments sufficient for their support, the expenses of which may be reduced to a very low rate individually, by arrangements which may be easily formed to supply all their wants with little trouble to themselves; and by their previous instruction they will be enabled to afford the small additional subscription which will be required for these purposes.

This part of the arrangement would always present a prospect of rest, comfort, and happiness to those employed: in consequence their daily occupations would be performed with more spirit and cheerfulness, and their labour would appear comparatively light and easy. Those still engaged in active operations would of course frequently visit their former companions and friends, who after having spent their years of toil were in the actual enjoyment of this simple retreat; and from this intercourse each party would naturally derive pleasure. The reflections of each would be most gratifying. The old would rejoice that they had been trained in habits of industry, temperance, and foresight, to enable them to receive and enjoy in their declining years every reasonable comfort which the present state of society will admit; the young and middle-aged, that they were pursuing the same course; and that they had not been trained to waste their money, time, and health, in idleness and intemperance.

These, then, are the plans which are in progress or intended for the further improvement of the inhabitants of New Lanark: they have uniformly proceeded from the principles which have been developed through these

Essays, restrained however, hitherto, in their operations by the local sentiments and unfounded notions of the community and neighbourhood, and by the peculiar circumstances of the establishment.

In every measure to be introduced at the place in question, for the comfort and happiness of man, the existing errors of the country were always to be considered; and as the establishment belonged to parties whose views were various, it became also necessary to devise means to create pecuniary gains from each improvement sufficient to satisfy the spirit of commerce.

All therefore which has been done for the happiness of this community, which consists of between two and three thousand individuals, is far short of what might have been easily effected in practice, had not mankind been previously trained in error. Hence, in devising these plans, the sole consideration was not what were the measures, dictated by these principles, which would produce the greatest happiness to man; but what could be effected in practice under the present irrational systems by which these proceedings were surrounded.

Imperfect however as these proceedings must yet be, in consequence of the formidable obstructions enumerated, they will yet appear, upon a full and minute investigation by minds equal to the comprehension of such a system, to combine a greater degree of substantial comfort to the individuals employed in the manufactory, and of pecuniary profit to the proprietors, than has hitherto been found attainable.

But to whom can such arrangements be submitted? Not to the mere commercial character, in whose estimation to forsake the path of immediate individual gain would be to show symptoms of a disordered imagination; for the children of commerce have been trained to direct all their faculties to buy cheap and sell dear; and consequently those who are the most expert and successful in this wise and noble art are in the commercial world deemed to possess foresight and superior acquirements, while such as attempt to improve the moral habits and increase the comforts of those whom they employ are termed wild enthusiasts.

Nor yet are they to be submitted to the mere men of the law; for they are necessarily trained to endeavour to make wrong appear right, or involve both in a maze of intricacies, and to legalize injustice. Nor to mere political leaders or their partisans; for they are embarrassed by the trammels of party, which mislead their judgement, and often constrain them to sacrifice the real well-being of the community and of themselves to an apparent but most mistaken self-interest.

Nor to those termed heroes and conquerors, or their followers; for their minds have been trained to consider the infliction of human misery, and the commission of military murders, a glorious duty, almost beyond reward.

Nor yet to the fashionable or splendid in their appearance; for these are from infancy trained to deceive and to be deceived; to accept shadows for substances; and to live a life of insincerity, and consequent discontent and misery.

Still less are they to be exclusively submitted to the official expounders and defenders of the various opposing religious systems throughout the world; for many of these are actively engaged in propagating imaginary notions, which cannot fail to vitiate the rational powers of man, and perpetuate his misery.

These principles therefore, and the practical systems which they recommend, are not to be submitted to the judgement of those who have been trained under and continue in any of these unhappy combinations of circumstances; but they are to be submitted to the dispassionate and patient investigation and decision of those individuals of every rank and class and denomination in society, who have become in some degree conscious of the errors in which they exist; who have felt the thick mental darkness by which they are surrounded; who are ardently desirous of discovering and following truth wherever it may lead; and who can perceive the inseparable connection which exists between individual and general, between private and public good!

It has been said, and it is now repeated, that these principles, thus combined, will prove themselves unerringly true against the most insidious or open attack; and ere long they will, by their irresistible truth, pervade society to the utmost bounds of the earth; for 'silence will not retard their progress, and opposition will give increased celerity to their movements'. When they shall have dissipated in some degree, as they speedily will dissipate, the thick darkness in which the human mind has been and still is enveloped, the endless beneficial consequences which must follow the general introduction of them into practice may then be explained in greater detail, and urged upon minds to which they will then appear less questionable. In the mean time we shall proceed to state, in a fourth Essay, of what immediate improvements the present state of the British population is susceptible in practice.

## ESSAY FOURTH

### *The Principles of the Former Essays applied to Government*

The end of government is to make the governed and the governors happy.

That government then is the best, which in practice produces the greatest happiness[44] to the greatest number; including those who govern, and those who obey.

If there be one duty therefore more imperative than another, on the government of every country, it is, that it should adopt, without delay, the proper means to form those sentiments and habits in the people, which shall give the most permanent and substantial advantages to the individuals and to the community.

And yet, with all the parade of learning contained in the myriads of volumes which have been written, and which still daily pour from the press, the knowledge of the first step of the progress which leads to human happiness remains yet unknown, or disregarded by the mass of mankind.

The important knowledge to which we allude is, 'That the old collectively may train the young collectively, to be ignorant and miserable, or to be intelligent and happy.' And, on investigation, this will be found to be one of those simple yet grand laws of the universe which experience discovers and confirms, and which, as soon as men become familiar with it, will no longer admit of denial or dispute. Fortunate will be that government which shall first acquire this knowledge in theory, and adopt it in practice.

To obtain its introduction into our own country first, a mode of procedure is now submitted to the immediate governing powers of the British Empire; and it is so submitted with an ardent desire that it may undergo the most full and ample discussion; that if it shall, as on investigation it will, be found to be the only consistent, and therefore rational, system of conducting human beings, it may be temperately and progressively introduced, instead of those defective national practices by which the state is now governed.

We therefore proceed to explain how this principle may now be introduced into practice, without injury to any part of society. For it is the time and manner of introducing this principle, and its consequent practice, which alone constitute any difficulty.

This will appear evident, when it is considered that, although, from a plain statement of the most simple facts, the truth of the principle cannot fail to prove so obvious that no one will ever attempt openly to attack it; and although its adoption into practice will speedily accumulate benefits of which the world can now form no adequate conception: yet both theory and practice are to be introduced into a society, trained and matured under principles that have impressed upon the individuals who compose it the most opposite habits and sentiments; which have been so entwined from infancy in their bodily and mental growth, that the simplicity and irresistible power of truth alone can disentangle them, and expose their fallacy. It becomes then necessary, to prevent the evils of a too sudden change, that those who have been thus nursed in ignorance may be progressively removed from the abodes of mental darkness, to the intellectual light which this principle cannot fail to produce.

To proceed on this plan, it becomes necessary to direct our attention to the actual state of the British population; to disclose the cause of those great and leading evils of which all now complain.

It will then be seen that the foundation on which these evils have been erected is ignorance, proceeding from the errors which have been impressed on the minds of the present generation by its predecessors; and chiefly by that greatest of all errors, the notion, that individuals form their own characters.

As a ground-work of a rational system, let this absurd doctrine, and all the chain of consequences which follow from it, be withdrawn, and let that only be taught as sacred, which can be demonstrated by its never-failing consistency to be true.

As a preliminary step, however, to the commencement of national improvements, it should be declared with a sincerity which shall not admit of any after deviation, that no individual of the present generation should be deprived of the emolument which he now receives, or of that which has been officially or legally promised.

The next step in national reform is to withdraw from the national church those tenets which constitute its weakness and create its danger. Yet still, to prevent the evils of any premature change, let the church in other respects remain as it is; because under the old established forms it may effect the most valuable purposes.

To render it truly a national church, all tests, as they are called, that is, declarations of belief in which all cannot conscientiously join, should be withdrawn: this alteration would tend more perhaps than any other which can be devised, to give stability both to the national church and to the state; and a conduct thus rational would at once terminate all the theological differences which now confound the intellects of men, and disseminate universal discord.

The next measure of national improvement should be to repeal or modify those laws which leave the lower orders in ignorance, train them to become intemperate, and produce idleness, gambling, poverty, disease, and murder. The production and consumption of ardent spirits are now legally encouraged; licenses to keepers of gin-shops and unnecessary pot-houses are by thousands annually distributed; the laws of the state now direct those licenses to be distributed; and yet perhaps not one of the authors or guardians of these laws has once reflected how much each of those houses daily contributes to public crime, disease, and weakness, or how much they add to the stock of private misery.

Let the duties therefore on the production of ardent spirits be gradually increased, until the price shall exceed the means of ordinary consumption; let the licenses be progressively withdrawn from the present occupiers of gin-shops and unnecessary pot-houses; and let the duties on the production and consumption of malt liquor be diminished, that the poor and working classes may be the more readily induced to abandon their destructive habits of dram-drinking, and by degrees to withdraw altogether from this incentive to crime, and source of misery.

The next measure for the general improvement of the British population should be to revise the laws relative to the poor.[45] For, pure and benevolent as, no doubt, were the motives which actuated those with whom the poor laws originated, the direct and certain effects of these laws are to injure the poor, and, through them, the state, as much almost as they can be injured.

They exhibit the appearance of affording aid to the

distressed, while, in reality, they prepare the poor to acquire the worst habits, and to practise every kind of crime; they thus increase the number of the poor, and add to their distress. It becomes therefore necessary that decisive and effectual measures should be adopted to remove those evils which the existing laws have created.

Benevolence says that the destitute must not starve, and to this declaration political wisdom readily assents. Yet can that system be right, which compels the industrious, temperate, and comparatively virtuous, to support the ignorant, the idle, and comparatively vicious? Such however is the effect of the present British poor-laws; for they publicly proclaim greater encouragement to idleness, ignorance, extravagance, and intemperance, than to industry and good conduct: the evils which arise from a system so irrational, are hourly experienced, and hourly increasing.

It thus becomes necessary that some counteracting remedy be immediately devised and applied; for, injurious as these laws are, it is obviously impracticable, in the present state of the British population, to annul at once a system to which so large a portion of the people has been taught to look for support.

The proper system to supersede these laws has been in part already explained, but we proceed to unfold it still more. It may be called 'A System for the Prevention of Crime, and the Formation of Human Character'; and under an established and well-intentioned government, it will be found more efficacious in producing public benefit than any of the laws now in existence.

The fundamental principle on which all these Essays proceed is, that 'Children collectively may be taught any sentiments and habits'; or, in other words, 'trained to acquire any character'.

It is of importance that this principle should be ever present in the mind, and that its truth should be established beyond even the shadow of doubt.

Compare the national character of each community with the laws and customs by which they are respectively governed, and, without an exception, the one will be found the archetype of the other.

Where, in former ages, the laws and customs established by Lycurgus[46] formed man into a model for martial exploits, and a perfect instrument for war, he is now trained, by other laws and customs, to be the instrument of a despotism which renders him almost or altogether unfit for war. And where the laws and customs of Athens trained the young mind to acquire as high a degree of partial rationality as the history of preceding times records; man is now reduced, by a total change of laws and customs, to the lowest state of mental degradation. Also where, formerly, the superior native American tribes roamed fearlessly through their trackless forests, uniformly exhibiting the hardy, penetrating, elevated, and sincere character, which was at a loss to comprehend how a rational being could desire to possess more than his nature could enjoy; now, on the very same soil, in the same climate, characters are formed under laws and customs so opposite, that all their bodily and mental faculties are individually exerted to obtain, if possible, ten thousand times more than any man can enjoy.

No one, it may be supposed, can now be so defective in knowledge as to imagine that it is a different human nature, which by its own power forms itself into a child of ignorance, of poverty, and of habits leading to crime and to punishment; or into a votary of fashion, claiming distinction from its folly and inconsistency; or to fancy that it is some undefined, blind, unconscious process of human nature itself, distinct from instruction, that forms the sentiments and habits of the men of commerce, of agriculture, the law, the church, the army, the navy, or of the private and illegal depredator on society; or that it is a different human nature which constitutes the societies of the Jews, of Friends, and of all the various religious denominations which have existed or which now exist. No! human nature, save the minute differences which are ever found in all the compounds of the creation, is one and the same in all; it is without exception universally plastic, and, by judicious training, the infants of any one class in the world may be readily formed into men of any other class; even to believe and declare that conduct to be right and virtuous, and to die in its defence, which their parents had been taught to believe and say was wrong and vicious, and to oppose which, those parents would also have willingly sacrificed their lives.

The kind and degree of misery or happiness experienced by the members of any community, depend on the characters which have been formed in the individuals which constitute the community. It follows that every state, to be well governed, ought to direct its chief attention to the formation of character; and that the best governed state will be that which shall possess the best national system of education.

Under the guidance of minds competent to its direction, a national system of training and education may be formed, to become the most safe, easy, effectual, and economical instrument of government that can be devised. And it may be made to possess a power equal to the accomplishment of the most grand and beneficial purposes.

It is, however, by instruction only that the population of the world can be made conscious of the irrational state in which they now exist; and until that instruction is given, it is premature to introduce a national system of education.

But the time is now arrived when the British Government may with safety adopt a national system of training and education for the poor and uninstructed; and this measure alone, if the plan shall be well devised and executed, will effect the most importantly beneficial changes.

As a preliminary step, however, it is necessary to observe, that to create a well trained, united, and happy people, this national system should be uniform over the United Kingdom; it should be also founded in the spirit of peace and of rationality; and for the most obvious reasons, the thought of exclusion to one child in the empire should not for a moment be entertained.

Several plans have been lately proposed for the national education of the poor, but these have not been calculated to effect all that a national system for the education of the poor ought to accomplish.

For the authors and supporters of these systems we feel those sentiments which the principles developed throughout these Essays must create in any minds on which they have been early and effectually impressed; and we are desirous of rendering their labours for the community as extensively beneficial as they can be made. To fulfil, however, a great and important public duty, the plans which they have devised must be considered as though they had been produced and published in the days of antiquity.

The plans alluded to are those of the Reverend Dr. Bell, Mr. Joseph Lancaster, and Mr. Whitbread.[47]

The systems of Dr. Bell and Mr. Lancaster, for instructing the poor in reading, writing, and arithmetic, prove the extreme ignorance which previously existed in the *manner* of training the young; for it is in the manner alone of giving instruction that these new systems are an improvement on the modes of instruction which were formerly practised.

The arrangement of the room, and many of the details in Mr. Lancaster's plan, are in some respects better calculated to give instruction in the elements enumerated, than those recommended by Dr. Bell, although some of the details introduced by the latter are very superior, and highly deserving of adoption.

The essence, however, of national training and education is to impress on the young, ideas and habits which shall contribute to the future happiness of the individual and of the state; and this can be accomplished only by instructing them to become rational beings.

It must be evident to common observers, that children may be taught, by either Dr. Bell's or Mr. Lancaster's system, to read, write, account, and sew, and yet acquire the worst habits, and have their minds rendered irrational for life.

Reading and writing are merely instruments, by which knowledge, either true or false, may be imparted; and, when given to children, are of little comparative value, unless they are also taught how to make a proper use of them.

When a child receives a full and fair explanation of the objects and characters around him, and when he is also taught to reason correctly, so that he may learn to discover general truths from falsehood; he will be much better instructed, although without the knowledge of one letter or figure, than those are who have been compelled to *believe*, and whose reasoning faculties have been confounded, or destroyed, by what is most erroneously termed learning.

It is readily acknowledged, that the manner of instructing children is of importance, and deserves all the attention which it has lately received; that those who discover or introduce improvements which facilitate the acquirement of knowledge, are important benefactors to their fellow-creatures. Yet the manner of giving instruction is one thing, the instruction itself another, and no two objects can be more distinct. The worst manner may be applied to give the best instruction, and the best manner to give the worst instruction. Were the real importance of both to be estimated by numbers, the manner of instruction may be compared to one, and the matter of instruction to millions; the first is the means only; the last, the end to be accomplished by those means.

If therefore, in a national system of education for the poor, it be desirable to adopt the best manner, it is surely so much the more desirable to adopt also the best matter, of instruction.

Either give the poor a rational and useful training, or mock not their ignorance, their poverty, and their misery, by merely instructing them to become conscious of the extent of the degradation under which they exist. And therefore, in pity to suffering humanity, either keep the poor, if you now can, in the state of the most abject ignorance, as near as possible to animal life; or at once determine to form them into rational beings, into useful and effective members of the state.

Were it possible, without national prejudice, to examine into the matter of instruction which is now given in some of our boasted new systems for the instruction of the poor, it would be found almost as wretched as any which can be devised. In proof of this statement, enter any one of the schools denominated national, request the master to show the acquirements of the children; these are called out, and he asks them theological questions to which men of the most profound erudition cannot make a rational reply: the children, however, readily answer as they had been previously instructed, for memory in this mockery of learning is all that is required.

Thus the child whose natural faculty of comparing ideas, or whose rational powers, shall be the soonest destroyed, if, at the same time, he possess a memory to retain incongruities without connexion, will become what is termed the first scholar in the class; and three fourths of the time which ought to be devoted to the acquirement of useful instruction, will be really occupied in destroying the mental powers of the children.

To those accustomed attentively to notice the human countenance, from infancy to age, in the various classes and religious denominations of the British population, it is truly an instructive although melancholy employment, to observe in the countenances of the poor children in these schools, the evident expression of mental injury derived from the well intentioned, but most mistaken, plan of their instruction.

Enough surely has now been said of the manner and matter of instruction in these new systems, to exhibit them in a just and true light.

The improvements in the manner of teaching children whatever may be deemed proper for them to learn; improvements which we may easily predict will soon receive great additions and amendments; have proceeded from the Reverend Dr. Bell and Mr. Lancaster;

while the errors which their respective systems assist to engrave on the ductile mind of infancy and childhood, are derived from times when ignorance gave countenance to every kind of absurdity.

Mr. Whitbread's scheme for the education of the poor, was evidently the production of an ardent mind possessing considerable abilities: his mind, however, had been irregularly formed by the errors of his early education; and was most conspicuous in the speech[48] which introduced the plan he had devised to the House of Commons, and in the plan itself.

The first was a clear exposition of all the reasons for the education of the poor, which could be expected from a human being trained from infancy under the systems in which Mr. Whitbread had been instructed.

The plan itself evinced the fallacy of the principles which he had imbibed, and showed that he had not acquired a practical knowledge of the feelings and habits of the poor, or of the only effectual means by which they could be trained to be useful to themselves and to the community.

Had Mr. Whitbread not been trained, as almost all the Members of both House of Parliament have been, in delusive theories devoid of rational foundation, which prevent them from acquiring an extensive practical knowledge of human nature, he would not have committed a plan for the national education of the poor to the sole management and direction of the Ministers, Churchwardens, and Overseers of Parishes, whose present interests must have appeared to be opposed to the measure.

He would surely first have devised a plan to make it the evident interest of the Ministers, Churchwardens, and Overseers, to co-operate in giving efficacy to the system which he wished to introduce to their super-intendence; and also to render them, by previous training, competent to that superintendence for which now they are in general unprepared. For, trained as these individuals have hitherto been, they must be deficient in the practical knowledge necessary to enable them successfully to direct the instruction of others. And had an attempt been made to carry Mr. Whitbread's plan into execution, it would have created a scene of confusion over the whole kingdom.

Attention to the subject will make it evident that it never was, and that it never can be, the interest of any sect claiming exclusive privileges on account of pro-fessing high and mysterious doctrines, about which the best and most conscientious men may differ in opinion, that the mass of the people should be otherwise in-structed than in those doctrines which were and are in unison with its peculiar tenets; and, that at this hour a national system of education for the lower orders on sound political principles is really dreaded, even by some of the most learned and intelligent members of the church of England. Such feelings in the members of the national church are those only which ought to be expected; for most men so trained and circumstanced must of necessity acquire those feelings. Why therefore should any class of men endeavour to rouse the indig-nation of the public against them? Their conduct and their motives are equally correct, and therefore equally good with those who raise the cry against and oppose the errors of the church. And let it ever be remembered, that an establishment which possesses the power of propagating principles, may be rendered truly valuable when directed to inculcate a system of self-evident truth, unobstructed by inconsistencies and counteractions.

The Dignitaries of the Church, and their adherents, foresaw that a national system for the education of the poor, unless it were placed under the immediate influence and management of individuals belonging to the church, would effectually and rapidly undermine the errors not only of their own, but of every other ecclesiastical establishment. In this foresight, they evinced the superiority of their penetration over the sectaries by whom the unexclusive system of education is supported. The heads of the church have wisely discovered that reason and inconsistency cannot long exist together; that the one must inevitably destroy the other, and reign paramount. They have witnessed the regular, and latterly the rapid progress which reason has made; they know that its accumulating strength cannot be much longer resisted; and as they now see the contest is hopeless, the unsuccessful attempt to destroy the Lancasterian System of Education is the last effort they will ever make to counteract the dissemination of knowledge, which is now widely extending itself in every direction.

The establishment of the Reverend Dr. Bell's system for initiating the children of the poor in all the tenets of the Church of England, is an attempt to ward off a little longer the yet dreaded period of a change from ignorance to reason; from misery to happiness.

Let us, however, not attempt impossibilities, the task is vain and hopeless; the church, while it adheres to the defective and injurious parts of its system, cannot be induced to act cordially in opposition to its apparent interests.

The principles here advocated will not admit the application of any deception to any class of men; they countenance no proceedings in practice, but of unlimited sincerity and candour; they give rise to no one sentiment which is not in unison with the happiness of the human race; and they impart knowledge, which renders it evident that such happiness can never be acquired, until every particle of falsehood and deception shall be eradicated from the instructions which the old force upon the young.

Let us then, in this spirit, openly declare to the church, that a national unexclusive plan of education for the poor will, without the shadow of doubt, destroy all the errors which are attached to the various systems; and that, when this plan shall be fully established, not one of the tenets which is in opposition to facts can long be upheld.

The wise and prudent then of all parties, instead of wishing to destroy national establishments, will use their utmost exertions to render them so consistent and reasonable in all their parts, that every well-disposed mind may be induced to give them their hearty and willing support.

To those who can reflect, and will attend to the passing scenes before them, the times are indeed awfully interesting; some change of high import, scarcely yet perhaps to be scanned by the present ill-taught race of men, is evidently in progress: in consequence, well founded, prompt, and decisive measures are now required in the British councils, to direct this change, and relieve the nation from the errors of its present systems.

It must surely then be the desire of every rational man, of every true friend to humanity, that a cordial co-operation and unity of action should be effected between the British Executive, the Parliament, the Church, and the People, to lay a broad and firm foundation for the future happiness of themselves and the world.

Say not, my countrymen, that such an event is impracticable; for, by adopting the evident means to form a rational character in man, there is a plain and direct road opened, which, if pursued, will render its accomplishment not only possible but certain. That road too will be found the most safe and pleasant that human beings have ever yet travelled. It leads direct to intelligence and true knowledge, and will show the boasted acquirements of Greece, of Rome, and of all antiquity, to be the mere weakness of mental infancy. Those who travel this road will find it so straight and well defined, that no one will be in danger of wandering from the right course. Nor is it yet a narrow or exclusive path; it admits of no exclusion, every colour of body and diversity of mind are freely and alike admitted. It is open to the human race, and it is broad and spacious enough to receive the whole, were they increased a thousand fold.

We will now show how these principles may be immediately and most advantageously introduced into general practice.

It has been said that 'the state which shall possess the best national system of education, will be the best governed'; and if the principle on which all the reasoning of these Essays is founded, be true, then is that sentiment also true. Yet (will future ages credit the fact?) to this day the British Government is without any national system of training and education, even for its millions of poor and uninstructed!! The formation of the mind and habits of its subjects is permitted to go on at random, often in the hands of those who are the most incompetent in the empire; and the result is, the gross ignorance and disunion which now every where abound!!

Instead of continuing such unwise proceedings, a national system for the training and education of the labouring classes ought to be immediately arranged; and, if judiciously devised, it may be rendered the most valuable improvement ever yet introduced into practice.

For this purpose, an act should be passed for the instruction of all the poor and labouring classes in the three kingdoms.

In this act provision should be made,

First,—For the appointment of proper persons to direct this new department of Government,[49] which will be found ultimately to prove the most important of all its departments: consequently, those individuals who possess the highest integrity, abilities, and influence in the state, should be appointed to its direction.

Second,—For the establishment of seminaries,[50] in which those individuals, who shall be destined to form the minds and bodies of the future subjects of these realms, should be well initiated in the art and matter of instruction.

This is, and ought to be considered, an office of the greatest practical trust and confidence in the empire; for let this duty be well performed, and the government must proceed with ease to the people, and high gratification to those who govern.

At present, there are not any individuals in the kingdom who have been trained to instruct the rising generation, as it is for the interest and happiness of all that it should be instructed. The training of those who are to form the future man becomes a consideration of the utmost magnitude: for, on due reflection, it will appear that instruction to the young must be, of necessity, the only foundation upon which the superstructure of society can be raised. Let this instruction continue to be left, as heretofore, to chance, and often to the most inefficient members of the community, and society must still experience the endless miseries which arise from such weak and puerile conduct. On the contrary, let the instruction to the young be well devised and well executed, and no subsequent proceedings in the state can be materially injurious. For it may truly be said to be a wonder-working power; one that merits the deepest attention of the legislature; with ease it may be used to train man into a dæmon of mischief to himself and all around him, or into an agent of unlimited benevolence.

Third,—For the establishment of seminaries over the United Kingdoms; to be conveniently placed, and of sufficient extent to receive all those who require instruction.

Fourth,—For supplying the requisite expenditure for the building and support of those seminaries.

Fifth,—For their arrangement on the plan, which, for the manner of instruction, upon a due comparison of the various modes now in practice, or which may be devised, shall appear to be the best.

Sixth,—For the appointment of proper masters to each of the schools. And,

Last,—The matter of instruction, both for body and mind, in these seminaries, should be substantially beneficial to the individuals, and to the state. For this is, or ought to be, the sole motive for the establishment of national seminaries.

These are the outlines of the provisions necessary to prepare the most powerful instrument of good that has ever yet been placed in the hands of man.

It has been shown that the governing powers of any country may easily and economically give its subjects just sentiments, and the best habits; and so long as this shall remain unattempted, governments will continue to neglect their most important duties, as well as interests. Such neglect now exists in Britain, where, in lieu of the governing powers making any effort to attain these inestimable benefits for the individuals belonging to the empire, they content themselves with the existence of laws, which must create sentiments and habits highly injurious to the welfare of the individuals and of the state.

Many of these laws, by their never-failing effects, speak in a language which no one can misunderstand; and say to the unprotected and untaught: Remain in ignorance, and let your labour be directed by that ignorance: for while you can procure what is sufficient to support life by such labour, although that life should be an existence in abject poverty, disease, and misery, we will not trouble ourselves with you, or any of your proceedings: when, however, you can no longer procure work, or obtain the means to support nature, then apply for relief to the parish; and you shall be maintained in idleness.

And in ignorance and idleness, even in this country, where manual labour is or always might be made valuable, hundreds of thousands of men, women, and children, are daily supported. No one acquainted with human nature will suppose that men, women, and children, can be long maintained in ignorance and idleness, without becoming habituated to crime.

Why then are there any idle poor in these kingdoms? Solely because so large a part of the population have been permitted to grow up to manhood in gross ignorance; and because, when they are, or easily may be, trained to be willing to labour, useful and productive employment has not been provided for them.

All men may, by judicious and proper laws and training, readily acquire knowledge and habits which will enable them, if they be permitted, to produce far more than they need for their support and enjoyment; and thus any population, in the fertile parts of the earth, may be taught to live in plenty and in happiness, without the checks of vice and misery.

Mr. Malthus[51] is however correct, when he says that the population of the world is ever adapting itself to the quantity of food raised for its support; but he has not told us how much more food an intelligent and industrious people will create from the same soil, than will be produced by one ignorant and ill-governed. It is however as one, to infinity.

It is not intended to propose that the British Government should now give direct employment to all its working population: on the contrary, it is confidently expected that a national system for the training and education of the poor, and lower orders, will be so effectual, that ere long they will all find employment sufficient to support themselves, except in cases of a great sudden depression in the demand for, and consequent depreciation in the value of, labour.

To prevent the crime and misery which ever follow these unfavourable fluctuations in the demand for and value of labour, it ought to be a primary duty of every government that sincerely interests itself in the well-being of its subjects, to provide perpetual employment of real national utility, in which all who apply may be immediately occupied.

The most obvious, and in the first place the best,

source perhaps of employment would be the making and repairing of roads.

In times of very limited demand for labour, it is truly lamentable to witness the distress which arises among the industrious for want of regular employment, and their customary wages. In these periods, innumerable applications are made to the Superintendants of extensive manual operations, to obtain any kind of employment by which a subsistence may be procured. Such applications are often made by persons who, in search of work, have travelled from one extremity of the island to the other!

During these attempts to be useful and honest, in the common acceptation of the terms, the families of such wandering individuals accompany them, or remain at home; in either case, they generally experience sufferings and privations which the gay and splendid will hesitate to believe it possible that human nature could endure.

Yet, after this extended and anxious endeavour to procure employment, the applicant often returns unsuccessful; he cannot, by his most strenuous exertions, procure an honest and independent existence: therefore, with intentions perhaps as good, and a mind as capable of great and benevolent actions as the remainder of his fellow men, he has no other resources left but to starve; apply to his parish for relief, and thus suffer the greatest degradation; or rely on his own native exertions, and, to supply himself and family with bread, resort to what are termed dishonest means.

Some minds thus circumstanced are so delicately formed that they will not accept the one, or adopt the other of the two latter modes to sustain life, and in consequence they actually starve. These, however, it is to be hoped, are not very numerous. But the number is undoubtedly great, of those whose health is ruined by bad and insufficient food, clothing, and shelter; who contract lingering diseases, and suffer premature death, the effect of partial starvation.

The most ignorant and least enterprising of them apply to the parish for support; soon lose the desire of exertion; become permanently dependent; conscious of their degradation in society; and henceforward, with their offspring, remain a burden and grievous evil to the state; while those among this class who yet possess strength and energy of body and mind, with some undestroyed powers of reasoning, perceive, in part, the glaring errors and injustice of society towards themselves and their fellow sufferers.

Can it then create surprise that feelings like those described should force human nature to endeavour to retaliate?

Multitudes of our fellow men are so goaded by these reflections and circumstances, as to be urged, even while incessantly and closely pursued by legal death, almost without a chance of escape, to resist those laws under which they suffer; and thus the private depredator on society is formed, fostered, and matured.

Shall we then longer withhold national instruction from our fellow men, who, it has been shown, might easily be trained to be industrious, intelligent, virtuous, and valuable members of the state?

True indeed it is, that all the measures now proposed are only a compromise with the errors of the present systems: but as these errors now almost universally exist, and must be overcome solely by the force of reason; and as reason, to effect the most beneficial purposes, makes her advance by slow degrees, and progressively substantiates one truth of high import after another, it will be evident to minds of comprehensive and accurate thought, that by these and similar compromises alone can success be rationally expected in practice. For such compromises bring truth and error before the public; and whenever they are fairly exhibited together, truth must ultimately prevail.

It is not however to be imagined, that this free and open exposure of the gross errors in which the existing generation has been instructed should be forthwith palatable to the world; it would be contrary to reason to form any such expectations.

Yet, as evil exists, and as man cannot be rational, nor of course happy, until the cause of it shall be removed; the writer, like a physician who feels the deepest interest in the welfare of his patient, has hitherto administered of this unpalatable restorative the smallest quantity which he deemed sufficient for the purpose: he now waits to see the effects which that may produce: should the application not prove of sufficient strength to remove the mental disorder, he promises that it shall be increased, until sound health to the public mind be firmly and permanently established.

# AN OUTLINE OF
# THE SYSTEM OF EDUCATION
# AT NEW LANARK

## by Robert Dale Owen[52]

Owen's eldest son published his account of the New Lanark schools in 1824, shortly before he, together with his father, became involved in the New Harmony venture. These few extracts show the range and quality of the activities in the schools.

The 'New Institution', or School, which is open for the instruction of the children and young people connected with the establishment, to the number of about 600, consists of two stories. The upper story, which is furnished with a double range of windows, one above the other, all round, is divided into two apartments; one, which is the principal school-room, fitted up with desks and forms, on the Lancasterian plan, having a free passage down the centre of the room, is about 90 feet long, 40 feet broad, and 20 feet high. It is surrounded, except at one end, where a pulpit stands, with galleries,[53] which are convenient, when this room is used, as it frequently is, either as a lecture room or place of worship.

The other apartment, on the second floor, is of the same width and height as that just mentioned, but only 49 feet long. The walls are hung round with representations of the most striking zoological and mineralogical specimens; including quadrupeds, birds, fishes, reptiles, insects, shells, minerals, &c. At one end there is a gallery, adapted for the purpose of an orchestra, and at the other are hung very large representations of the two hemispheres; each separate country, as well as the various seas, islands, &c. being differently coloured, but without any names attached to them. This room is used as a lecture and ball-room, and it is here, that the dancing and singing lessons are daily given. It is likewise occasionally used as a reading room for some of the classes.

The lower story is divided into three apartments, of nearly equal dimensions, 12 feet high, and supported by hollow iron pillars, serving, at the same time, as conductors, in winter, for heated air, which issues through the floor of the upper story, and by which means the whole building may, with ease, be kept at any required temperature. It is in these three apartments that the younger classes are taught reading, natural history, and geography.

We may here remark, that it is probable, the facility of teaching the older classes particularly, would have been greatly increased, had some part of the building been divided into smaller apartments, appropriating one to each class of from twenty to thirty children, provided such an arrangement had not encroached either on the lecture room, or principal school-room.

Each of the two elder classes for the boys, and the same for the girls, who at that age are taught reading, writing, &c. separately from the boys, and only meet them during the lectures, and in the lessons in singing and dancing, consists of from twenty to forty children. The younger classes, composed indiscriminately of boys and girls, are rather more numerous. A master is appointed to each class. There are likewise, attached to the institution, a master who teaches dancing and singing, a drilling master, and a sewing mistress.

At present the older classes are taught reading, writing, &c. in different parts of the principal school-room, the size of which prevents any confusion from such an arrangement; but, as was before observed, the facility with which their attention could be gained, would probably be greatly increased, could a separate apartment be appropriated to each class. The very size of the room, too, increases the difficulty, of itself no slight one, of modulating the voice in reading.

The hours of attendance, in the day school, are from half past seven till nine, from ten till twelve, and from three till five in the afternoon. In winter, however, instead of coming to school again in the afternoon from three to five, the children remain, with an interval of half an hour, from ten till two o'clock, when they are dismissed for the day; making the same number of hours in summer and winter.

The ages of the children are from eighteen months to ten or sometimes twelve years. They are allowed to remain at school as long as their parents will consent to their doing so; though the latter generally avail themselves of the permission which is granted them, to send their children into the manufactory at ten years of age, or soon after. It is the wish of the founder of these schools, that the parents should not require their children to attend a stated employment till they are at least twelve years old; and it cannot admit of a doubt, that the general adoption of such a measure would be productive of the most important advantages to the parents themselves, to the children, and to society at large.

The infant classes, from two to five years, remain in school only one half of the time mentioned as the regular hours of attendance for the other classes. During the remainder of the time, they are allowed to amuse themselves at perfect freedom, in a large paved area in front of the Institution, under the charge of a young woman, who finds less difficulty—and without harshness or punishment—in taking charge of, and rendering contented and happy, one hundred of these little creatures than most individuals, in a similar situation, experience in conducting a nursery of two or three children. By this means, these infants acquire healthful and hardy habits; and are, at the same time, trained to associate in a kind and friendly manner with their little companions; thus practically learning the pleasure to be derived from such conduct, in opposition to envious bickerings, or ill-natured disputes.

The school is open in the evening to the children and young persons, from 10 to 20 years of age; the system pursued with them is so similar to that adopted in the day school, that in describing the one, we shall give an accurate idea of the other also.

The dress worn by the children in the day school, both boys and girls, is composed of strong white cotton cloth, of the best quality that can be procured. It is formed in the shape of the Roman tunic,[54] and reaches, in the boys dresses, to the knee, and in those of the girls, to the ancle. These dresses are changed three times a week, that they may be kept perfectly clean and neat.

The parents of the older children pay 3d. a month for their instruction. Nothing is paid for the infant classes, or for the evening scholars. This charge is intended merely to prevent them from regarding the Institution with the feelings connected with a charity school. It does not amount to one-twentieth part of the expenses of the school, which is supported by the proprietors of the establishment.

It has been deemed necessary, in order to meet the

wishes of the parents, to commence teaching the children the elements of reading, at a very early age; but it is intended that this mode should, ultimately, be superseded, at least until the age of seven or eight, by a regular course of natural history, geography, ancient and modern history, chemistry, astronomy, &c. on the principle, that it is following the plan prescribed by nature, to give a child such particulars as he can easily be made to understand, concerning the nature and properties of the different objects around him, before we proceed to teach him the artificial signs which have been adopted to represent these objects. It is equally impolitic and irrational, at once to disgust him by a method to him obscure or unintelligible, and consequently tedious and uninteresting, of obtaining that knowledge, which may, in the meantime, be agreeably communicated by conversation, and illustrated by sensible signs; and which may thus, by giving the child a taste for learning, render the attainments of reading and writing really interesting to him, as the means of conferring increased facilities, in acquiring further information.

The following are the branches of instruction at present taught at New Lanark.

### Reading

Great difficulty has been experienced, in procuring proper school books for the different classes. Those at present in use, are in many respects defective: they are but ill adapted to the capacities of children so young, and are consequently not calculated to interest them sufficiently. An exception to this last observation must however be made in favour of Miss Edgeworth's[55] little works; but even these contain too much of praise and blame, to admit of their being regarded as unexceptionable. From some little volumes of voyages and travels, too, illustrated by plates and maps, and interspersed with amusing and characteristic anecdotes, great assistance has been derived. The elder classes have often only one copy of each work, from which one of their number reads aloud to the others, who are generally questioned, after a few sentences have been read, as to the substance of what they have just heard. In their answers, they are not confined to the author's words; on the contrary, their answering in a familiar manner, and employing such expressions, as they themselves best understand, is considered as a proof, that they have attended more to the sense, than to the sound.

The general principle, that children should never be directed to read what they cannot understand, has been found to be of the greatest use.

The children are taught to read according to the sense, and, as nearly as possible, as they would speak; so as, at once, to show, that they comprehend what they are reading, and to give their companions an opportunity of comprehending it likewise. In order to teach them the proper tone and modulation of the voice, the master frequently reads to his class some interesting work; he then allows his pupils to ask any questions, or make any remarks, that may occur to them.

### *Writing*

The mode of teaching writing, is, in the commencement, nearly the same as that adopted in most schools; but as soon as the children can write a tolerably fair text copy, the master begins to teach them current hand writing, according to a plan which has been lately adopted in various seminaries. By this method the children write without lines; and with a little attention, soon learn to correct the stiff formal school hand, generally written, into a fair, legible business hand, such as shall be useful to them in after life.

The writing copies consist of short sentences, generally illustrative of some subject connected with history or geography; and the pupils finally proceed to copy from dictation, or from a book or manuscript, any passage that may be considered as difficult, and at the same time important to be retained in their memory. Thus, as soon as possible, applying the newly acquired medium of instruction in the most efficacious manner.

### Arithmetic

Has hitherto been taught on the system which commonly prevails in Scotland. The elder classes, however, are just beginning a regular course of mental arithmetic, similar to that adapted by M. Pestalozzi[56] of Iverdun in Switzerland. In this, as in every other department of instruction, the pupils are taught to understand what they are doing; the teacher explains to them why the different operations, if performed as directed, must be correct; and in what way the knowledge they are acquiring, may be beneficially employed in after life.

### Sewing

All the girls, except those in the two youngest classes, are taught sewing, including knitting, marking, cutting out, &c. One day of the week is appointed, when they are desired to bring to school any of their garments (which must previously have been washed) that may require mending, and these they are taught to repair as neatly as possible.

## Natural History, Geography, and Ancient and Modern History

These studies are classed together, because, though distinct in themselves, and embracing, each of them, so great a fund of information, they are taught at New Lanark nearly in the same manner; that is to say, in familiar lectures, delivered extempore, by the teachers. These lectures are given in classes of from 40 to 50. The children are subsequently examined regarding what they have heard; by which means the teacher has an opportunity of ascertaining, whether each individual pupil be in possession of the most important part of the lecture which he has attended. In these lectures, material assistance is derived from the use of sensible signs, adapted to the subject, and which we shall explain more particularly in their place. Each master selects a particular branch, and delivers, as has already been stated, a short lecture to 40 or 50 children at once. The number was formerly from 120 to 150 in one class; but this was found much too large, and one half or one third of that number is as many as it is found expedient to assemble together, except when the lecture is so interesting, as at once to rivet every child's attention, and so easily understood, as to require no subsequent explanation whatever.

Natural History is taught to all the scholars, even to the youngest, or infant classes; who can understand and become interested in a few simple particulars regarding such domestic animals as come under their own observation, if these are communicated in a sufficiently familiar manner; for this, indeed, is almost the first knowledge which Nature directs an infant to acquire.

In commencing a course of Natural History, the division of Nature into the Animal, Vegetable, and Mineral Kingdoms, is first explained to them, and in a very short time they learn at once to distinguish to which of these any object which may be presented to them, belongs. The teacher then proceeds to details of the most interesting objects furnished by each of these kingdoms, including descriptions of quadrupeds, birds, fishes, reptiles, and insects—and of the most interesting botanical and mineralogical specimens. These details are illustrated by representations of the objects, drawn on a large scale, and as correctly as possible. It is desirable, that these representations should be all on the same scale; otherwise the child's idea of their relative size becomes incorrect. These drawings may be either hung round the room, or painted, as the botanical representations at New Lanark are, on glazed canvass, which is rolled from one cylinder to another, both cylinders being fixed on an upright frame, at about six or eight feet distance from each other, so as to show only that length of canvass at once. These cylinders are turned by means of a handle, which may be applied to the one, or to the other, as the canvass is to be rolled up or down.

The classes are subsequently, individually, encouraged to repeat what they have heard, to express their opinions on it freely, and to ask any explanation.

In commencing a course of Geography, the children are taught the form of the earth, its general divisions into Land and Water, the subdivisions of the land into four Continents, and into larger and smaller Islands, that of the water into Oceans, Seas, Lakes, &c.; then the names of the principal countries, and of their capitals, together with the most striking particulars concerning their external appearance, natural curiosities, manners and customs, &c. &c. The different countries are compared with our own, and with each other.

The minds of the children are thus opened, and they are prevented from contracting narrow, exclusive notions, which might lead them to regard those only as proper objects of sympathy and interest, who may live in the same country with themselves—or to consider that alone as right, which they have been accustomed to see—or to suppose those habits and those opinions to be the standard of truth and of perfection, which the circumstances of their birth and education have rendered their own. In this manner are the circumstances, which induce national peculiarities and national vices, exhibited to them; and the question will naturally arise in their minds: 'Is it not highly probably that we ourselves, had we lived in such a country, should have escaped neither its peculiarities, nor its vices—that we should have adopted the notions and prejudices there prevalent? in fact is it not evident, that we might have been Cannibals or Hindoos, just as the circumstance of our birth should have placed us, in Hindoostan, where the killing of an animal becomes a heinous crime; or amongst some savage tribe, where to torture a fellow creature, and to feast on his dead body, is accounted a glorious action?' A child who has once felt what the true answer to such a question must be, cannot remain uncharitable or intolerant.

Any one of the older classes at New Lanark, on being told the latitude and longitude of a place, can at once point it out; can say in what zone it is situated, and whether therefore, from its situation, it is a hot or a cold country—what is the number of degrees of latitude and longitude between it, and any other given country, even though on the opposite hemisphere; together, probably, with other details regarding the country; as for instance, whether it is fertile, or a desert; what is the colour and general character, and what the religion of its inhabitants; what animals are found there; when, and by whom it was discovered; what is the shortest way from England to that country; what is the name of the capital city, and of the principal mountains and rivers; and perhaps relate something of its history.

In the course of the lectures, numerous opportunities present themselves to communicate much general information, not strictly connected with the branches themselves, as for example, descriptions of natural phenomena, of trades, manufactures, &c. Thus, in short, furnishing them with whatever is useful or pleasant, or interesting for them to know.

Ancient and Modern History constitutes another branch of their education. It may be thought, that in teaching History, the aid of sensible signs can be but seldom called in. The reverse, however, is the case. Their application here is, in fact, more complete than in any other branch. Seven large maps or tables, laid out on the principle of the Stream of Time, and which were originally purchased from Miss Whitwell,[57] a lady who formerly conducted a respectable seminary in London —are hung round a spacious room. These, being made of canvass, may be rolled up at pleasure. On the Streams, each of which is differently coloured, and represents a nation, are painted the principal events which occur in the history of those nations. Each century is closed by a horizontal line, drawn across the map. By means of these maps, the children are taught the outlines of Ancient and Modern History, with ease to themselves, and without being liable to confound different events, or different nations. On hearing of any two events, for instance, the child has but to recollect the situation, on the tables, of the paintings, by which these are represented, in order to be furnished at once with their chronological relation to each other.

The intimate connexion between Natural History, Geography, and History, is evident, so that in lecturing on one of these subjects, the teacher finds many opportunities of recalling to the minds of his pupils various portions of the others.

### Religion

The founder of the schools at New Lanark has been accused of bringing up the children without religion.

The direct and obvious tendency of the whole system of education there, most fully warrants, as it appears to us, a representation the very reverse of this.

An acquaintance with the works of the Deity, such as these children acquire, must lay the basis of true religion. The uniform consistency of such evidence, all nations, and all sects, at once acknowledge. No diversity of opinion can exist with regard to it. It is an evidence with which every one who is really anxious that his children should adopt a true religion, must wish them to become acquainted; whether he may have been born in a Christian country, or be a disciple of Mahomet, or a follower of Bramah. Because simple facts can never mislead, or prejudice the mind. He who hesitates to receive them as the basis of his religion, tacitly acknowledges its inconsistency.

Even supposing a child instructed in true religion, and believing it implicitly, without, however, having acquired that belief by deducing its truth from known or well accredited facts,—upon what foundation can such a belief be said to rest? The first sceptic he may converse with, will probably excite a doubt of its truth in his mind; and he himself, being unable to defend his opinions, and having no means of reasoning on the subject, may soon become a violent opposer of that religion, which, though true, had yet been taught to him before he had acquired sufficient knowledge to understand its evidence, or was capable of judging of its truth or falsehood.

In any other study, the inconsistency of expecting the pupils to deduce correct conclusions before the facts upon which the reasoning proceeds, are known to them, would be glaringly evident.

And on this principle it is considered, that a child, at an early age, should become acquainted with facts, instead of being instructed in abstruse doctrinal points. If it often requires all the powers of the most matured human reason to decide on these points, surely we do wrong to present any of them to the minds of children.

At New Lanark, every opportunity is embraced of inculcating those practical moral principles which religion enjoins; and of storing the minds of the children, with the most important and striking natural facts; but the consideration of any abstruse doctrines is, as far as the religious views of the parents will admit, reserved for an age, when the pupils shall be better fitted to judge for themselves.

Before concluding this important subject, it may be necessary to say that the scriptures are and have always been statedly read, and the catechism regularly taught there—because this has been done, not as being considered the proper method of conveying religious instruction to the minds of young children, but because the parents were believed to wish it; and any encroachment on perfect liberty of conscience, was regarded as the worst species of tyrannical assumption.

Besides the studies already mentioned, the children are instructed in music and dancing; which are found essentially to contribute towards moral refinement, and improvement. When properly conducted, each of these acquirements becomes a pure and natural source of enjoyment; it is a well authenticated fact, that the best method of making a people virtuous, is to begin by rendering their situation comfortable and happy.

### *Singing*

All the children above five or six years of age are taught singing, sometimes by the ear, sometimes by the notes. They begin by learning the names and sounds of the notes, and by singing the gamut; then proceed to strike the distances, and finally acquire such a knowledge of the elements of the science of music, as they may easily reduce to practice. The musical notes and signs, as well as a variety of musical exercises, are represented on a large scale, on a rolled canvass, similar to that on which we have mentioned, that the botanical specimens are painted. A small selection of simple airs is made, for the school, every three months. The words to these are printed on sheets, one of which is given to each child. Spirited songs, in the bravura style, are found to be much more adapted to children under ten years of age, than more slow and pathetic airs; into the spirit of which they seldom seem to enter, while the former are uniformly their favourite songs, particularly any lively national airs with merry words. Almost all the children show more or less taste for music; although of course this appears in one child spontaneously, while in another it requires considerable cultivation.

The vocal performers in the evening school are sometimes joined by the instrumental band, belonging to the village. This recurs in general once a week.

### Dancing

Is taught, as a pleasant, healthful, natural and social exercise, calculated to improve the carriage and deportment, and to raise the spirits, and increase the cheerfulness and hilarity of those engaged in it. The dances are varied. Scotch reels, country dances, and quadrilles are danced in succession; and by some of the older pupils with a simple and unaffected ease and elegance, which we have never seen surpassed in children of their age.

Besides dancing, the children, boys and girls, now and then go through a few military evolutions, as well to give them the habit of marching regularly from place to place, as to improve their carriage and manner of walking. This species of exercise is never continued long at a time; and stiffness and unnecessary restraint are avoided as much as possible; on the principle, already mentioned, and which pervades the whole of the arrangements in these schools, that whatever is likely to prove unpleasant or irksome to the children, and is not necessary for the preservation of good order, or for some other useful purpose, should never be required of them. At the same time, whatever is really necessary to the proper regulation of the school, is uniformly but mildly enforced.

The general appearance of the children is to a stranger very striking. The leading character of their countenances is a mixed look of openness, confidence and intelligence, such as is scarcely to be met with among children in their situation. Their animal spirits are always excellent. Their manners and deportment towards their teachers and towards strangers, are fearless and unrestrained, yet neither forward, nor disrespectful. Their general health is so good, that the surgeon attached to the village, who is in the habit of examining the day scholars periodically, states, as the result of an examination, which took place a few weeks since; that, out of 300 children, only three had some slight complaint; and that all the others were in perfect health. The individual literary acquirements of the greater proportion of the older classes, are such as perhaps no body of children of the same age, in any situation, have had an opportunity of attaining. The writer of the present article has had frequent opportunities of examining them individually; and he has no hesitation in saying, that their knowledge on some of the subjects, which have been mentioned, as forming part of their instruction, is superior to his own.

A sufficient degree of friendly emulation is excited amongst them, without any artificial stimulus; but it is an emulation, which induces them to prefer going forward with their companions, to leaving them behind. Their own improvement is not their only source of enjoyment. That of their companions they appear to witness with pleasure, unmixed with any envious feeling whatever; and to be eager to afford them any assistance they may require.

# REPORT

*To the County of Lanark, of a Plan for relieving Public Distress and Removing Discontent, by giving permanent, productive Employment to the Poor and Working Classes, under Arrangements which will essentially improve their Character, and ameliorate their Condition, diminish the Expenses of Production and Consumption, and create Markets co-extensive with Production*

Owen first elaborated his proposals for the settlement of the unemployed in self-supporting communities early in 1817. This Report, drawn up in 1820 at the request of the County of Lanark, was his fullest statement of the economic and social implications of these proposals. A large amount of material not immediately relevant here (e.g. on currency) has been omitted.

The evil for which your Reporter has been required to provide a remedy, is the general want of employment, at wages sufficient to support the family of a working man beneficially for the community.

After the most earnest consideration of the subject he has been compelled to conclude that such employment cannot be procured through the medium of trade, commerce, or manufactures, or even of agriculture, until the Government and the Legislature, cordially supported by the country, shall previously adopt measures to remove obstacles, which, without their interference, will now permanently keep the working classes in poverty and discontent, and gradually deteriorate all the resources of the empire.

Your Reporter has been impressed with the truth of this conclusion by the following considerations:—

1st.—That manual labour, properly directed, is the source of all wealth,[58] and of national prosperity.

2nd.—That, when properly directed, labour is of far more value to the community than the expense necessary to maintain the labourer in considerable comfort.

3rd.—That manual labour, properly directed, may be made to continue of this value in all parts of the world, under any supposable increase of its population, for many centuries to come.

4th.—That, under a proper direction of manual labour, Great Britain and its dependencies may be made to support an incalculable increase of population, most advantageously for all its inhabitants.

5th.—That when manual labour shall be so directed, it will be found that population cannot, for many years, be stimulated to advance as rapidly as society might be benefited by its increase.

These considerations, deduced from the first and most obvious principles of the science of political economy, convinced your Reporter that some formidable artificial obstacle intervened to obstruct the natural improvement and progress of society.

It is well known that, during the last half century in particular, Great Britain, beyond any other nation, has progressively increased its powers of production, by a rapid advancement in scientific improvements and arrangements, introduced, more or less, into all the departments of productive industry throughout the empire.

The amount of this new productive power cannot, for want of proper data, be very accurately estimated; but your Reporter has ascertained from facts which none will dispute, that its increase has been enormous; —that, compared with the manual labour of the whole population of Great Britain and Ireland, it is, at least, as forty to one, and may be easily made as 100 to one; and that this increase may be extended to other countries; that it is already sufficient to saturate the world with wealth, and that the power of creating wealth may be made to advance perpetually in an accelerating ratio.

It appeared to your Reporter that the natural effect of the aid thus obtained from knowledge and science should be to add to the wealth and happiness of society in proportion as the new power increased and was judiciously directed; and that, in consequence, all parties would thereby be substantially benefited. All know, however, that these beneficial effects do not exist. On the contrary, it must be acknowledged that the working classes, which form so large a proportion of the population, cannot obtain even the comforts which their labour formerly procured for them, and that no party appears to gain, but all to suffer, by their distress.

Your Reporter directed his attention to the consideration of the possibility of devising arrangements by means of which the whole population might participate in the benefits derivable from the increase of scientific productive power.

This part of the Report naturally divides itself under the following heads, each of which shall be considered separately, and the whole, afterwards, in connection, as forming an improved practical system for the working classes, highly beneficial, in whatever light it may be viewed, to every part of society.

1st.—The number of persons who can be associated to give the greatest advantages to themselves and to the community.

2nd.—The extent of the land to be cultivated by such association.

3rd.—The arrangements for feeding, lodging, and clothing the population, and for training and educating the children.

4th.—Those for forming and superintending the establishments.

5th.—The disposal of the surplus produce, and the relation which will subsist between the several establishments.

6th.—Their connection with the government of the country and with general society.

The first object, then, of the political economist, in forming these arrangements, must be, to consider well under what limitation of numbers, individuals should be associated to form the first nucleus or division of society.

All his future proceedings will be materially influenced by the decision of this point, which is one of the most difficult problems in the science of political economy. It will affect essentially the future character of individuals, and influence the general proceedings of mankind.

Your Reporter ventures to recommend the formation of such arrangements as will unite about 300 men, women, and children, in their natural proportions, as the minimum, and about 2,000 as the maximum, for the future associations of the cultivators of the soil, who will be employed also in such additional occupations as may be advantageously annexed to it.

In coming to this conclusion your Reporter never lost sight of that only sure guide to the political economist, the principle, that it is the interest of all men, whatever may be their present artificial station in society, that there should be the largest amount of intrinsically valuable produce created, at the least expense of labour, and in a way the most advantageous to the producers and society.

It is with reference to this principle that the minimum and maximum above stated (viz. 300 and 2,000,) have been fixed upon, as will be more particularly developed under the subsequent heads.

Within this range more advantages can be given to the individuals and to society, than by the association of any greater or lesser number.

But from 800 to 1,200 will be found the most desirable number to form into agricultural villages; and unless some very strong local causes interfere, the permanent arrangements should be adapted to the complete accommodation of that amount of population only.

Villages of this extent, in the neighbourhood of others of a similar description, at due distances, will be found capable of combining within themselves all the advantages that city and country residences now afford, without any of the numerous inconveniences and evils which necessarily attach to both those modes of society.

But a very erroneous opinion will be formed of the proposed arrangements and the social advantages which they will exhibit, if it should be imagined from what has been said that they will in any respect resemble any of the present agricultural villages of Europe, or the associated communities in America,[59] except in so far as the latter may be founded on the principle of united labour, expenditure, and property, and equal privileges.

2nd—The extent of land to be cultivated by such association.

This will depend upon the quality of the soil and other local considerations.

Great Britain and Ireland, however, do not possess a population nearly sufficient to cultivate our best soils in the most advantageous manner. It would therefore be nationally impolitic to place these associations upon inferior lands, which, in consequence, may be dismissed from present consideration.

Society, ever misled by closet theorists, has committed almost every kind of error in practice, and in no instance perhaps a greater, than in separating the workman from his food, and making his existence depend upon the labour and uncertain supplies of others, as is the case under our present manufacturing system; and it is a vulgar error to suppose that a single individual more can be supported by means of such a system than without it; on the contrary, a whole population engaged in agriculture, with manufactures as an appendage, will, in a given district, support many more, and in a much higher degree of comfort, than the same district could do with its agricultural separate from its manufacturing population.

Improved arrangements for the working classes will, in almost all cases, place the workman in the midst of his food, which it will be as beneficial for him to create as to consume.

Sufficient land, therefore, will be allotted to these cultivators to enable them to raise an abundant supply of food and the necessaries of life for themselves, and as much additional agricultural produce as the public demands may require from such a portion of the population.

Under a well devised arrangement for the working classes they will all procure for themselves the necessaries and comforts of life in so short a time, and so easily and pleasantly, that the occupation will be experienced to be little more than a recreation, sufficient to keep them in the best health and spirits for rational enjoyment of life.

The surplus produce from the soil will be required only for the higher classes, those who live without manual labour, and those whose nice manual operations will not permit them at any time to be employed in agriculture and gardening.

Of the latter, very few, if any, will be necessary, as mechanism may be made to supersede such operations, which are almost always injurious to health.

Under this view of the subject, the quantity of land which it would be the most beneficial for these associations to cultivate, with reference to their own well-being and the interests of society, will probably be from half an acre to an acre and a half for each individual.

An association, therefore, of 1,200 persons, would require from 600 to 1,800 statute acres, according as it may be intended to be more or less agricultural.

Thus, when it should be thought expedient that the chief surplus products should consist in manufactured commodities, the lesser quantity of land would be sufficient; if a large surplus from the produce of the soil were deemed desirable, the greater quantity would be allotted; and when the localities of the situation should render it expedient for the association to create an equal surplus quantity of each, the medium quantity, or 1,200 acres, would be the most suitable.

It follows that land under the proposed system of husbandry would be divided into farms of from 150 to 3,000 acres, but generally perhaps from 800 to 1,500 acres. This division of the land will be found to be productive of incalculable benefits in practice; it will give all the advantages, without any of the disadvantages of small and large farms.

3rd.—The arrangement for feeding, lodging, and clothing the population, and for training and educating the children.

It being always most convenient for the workman to reside near to his employment, the site for the dwellings of the cultivators will be chosen as near to the centre of the land, as water, proper levels, dry situation &c., &c., may admit; and as courts, alleys, lanes, and streets create many unnecessary inconveniences, are injurious to health, and destructive to almost all the natural comforts of human life, they will be excluded, and a disposition of the buildings free from these objections and greatly more economical will be adopted.

As it will afterwards appear that the food for the whole population can be provided better and cheaper under one general arrangement of cooking, and that the children can be better trained and educated together under the eye of their parents than under any other circumstances, a large square, or rather parallelogram, will be found to combine the greatest advantages in its form for the domestic arrangements of the association.

The four sides of this figure may be adapted to contain all the private apartments or sleeping and sitting rooms for the adult part of the population; general sleeping apartments for the children while under tuition; store-rooms, or warehouses in which to deposit various products; an inn, or house for the accommodation of strangers; an infirmary; &c., &c.

In a line across the centre of the parallelogram, leaving

free space for air and light and easy communication, might be erected the church, or places for worship; the schools; kitchen and apartments for eating; all in the most convenient situation for the whole population, and under the best possible public superintendence, without trouble, expense, or inconvenience to any party.

The parallelogram being found to be the best form in which to dispose the dwelling and chief domestic arrangements for the proposed associations of cultivators, it will be useful now to explain the principles on which those arrangements have been formed.

The first in order, and the most necessary, are those respecting food.

It has been, and still is, a received opinion among theorists in political economy, that man can provide better for himself, and more advantageously for the public, when left to his own individual exertions, opposed to and in competition with his fellows, than when aided by any social arrangement which shall unite his interests individually and generally with society.

This principle of individual interest, opposed as it is perpetually to the public good, is considered, by the most celebrated political economists, to be the corner-stone to the social system, and without which, society could not subsist.

Yet when they shall know themselves, and discover the wonderful effects which combination and union can produce, they will acknowledge that the present arrangement of society is the most anti-social, impolitic, and irrational, that can be devised.

From this principle of individual interest have arisen all the divisions of mankind, the endless errors and mischiefs of class, sect, party, and of national antipathies, creating the angry and malevolent passions, and all the crimes and misery with which the human race have been hitherto afflicted.

In short, if there be one closet doctrine more contrary to truth than another, it is the notion that individual interest, as that term is now understood, is a more advantageous principle on which to found the social system, for the benefit of all, or of any, than the principle of union and mutual co-operation.

Men have not yet been trained in principles that will permit them to act in union, except to defend themselves or to destroy others. For self-preservation they were early compelled to unite for these purposes in war. A necessity, however, equally powerful, will now compel men to be trained to act together to create and conserve, that, in like manner, they may preserve life in peace. Fortunately for mankind the system of individual opposing interests has now reached the extreme point of error and inconsistency;—in the midst of the most ample means to create wealth, all are in poverty, or in imminent danger from the effects of poverty upon others.

The reflecting part of mankind have admitted, in theory, that the characters of men are formed chiefly by the circumstances in which they are placed; yet the science of the influence of circumstances, which is the most important of all the sciences, remains unknown for the great practical business of life.

The discovery of the distance and movements of the heavenly bodies,—of the time-piece,—of a vessel to navigate the most distant parts of the ocean,—of the steam-engine, which performs under the easy control of one man the labour of many thousands,—and of the press, by which knowledge and improvement may be speedily given to the most ignorant in all parts of the earth,—these have, indeed, been discoveries of high import to mankind; but, important as these and others have been in their effects on the condition of human society, their combined benefits in practice will fall far short of those which will be speedily attained by the new intellectual power which men will acquire through the knowledge of 'the science of the influence of circumstances over the whole conduct, character, and proceedings of the human race'.

Your Reporter knows that the full development of these truths is absolutely necessary to prepare the public to receive and understand the practical details which he is about to explain. He is not now, however, addressing the common public, but those whose minds have had all the benefit of the knowledge which society at present affords; and it is from such individuals that he hopes to derive the assistance requisite to effect the practical good which he has devoted all the powers and faculties of his mind to obtain for his fellow-creatures.

Your Reporter has stated that this happy change will be effected through the knowledge which will be derived from the science of the influence of circumstances over human nature.

Through this science, new mental powers will be created, which will place all those circumstances that determine the misery or happiness of men under the immediate control and direction of the present population of the world. This science may be truly called one whereby ignorance, poverty, crime, and misery, may be prevented; and will indeed open a new era to the human race; one in which real happiness will commence, and perpetually go on increasing through every succeeding generation.

It is now time to return to the consideration of the preparatory means by which these important results are to be accomplished.

Your Reporter now uses the term 'preparatory', because the present state of society, governed by circumstances, is so different, in its several parts and entire combination, from that which will arise when society shall be taught to govern circumstances, that some temporary intermediate arrangements, to serve as a step whereby we may advance from the one to the other, will be necessary.

The long experience which he has had in the practice of the science now about to be introduced has convinced him of the utility, nay, of the absolute necessity, of forming arrangements for a temporary intermediate stage of existence, in which we, who have acquired the wretched habits of the old system, may be permitted, without inconvenience, gradually to part with them, and exchange them for those requisite for the new and improved state of society. The habits, dispositions, notions, and consequent feelings, engendered by old society, will be thus allowed, without disturbance of any kind, to die a natural death.

Under the present system there is the most minute division of mental power and manual labour in the individuals of the working classes; private interests are placed perpetually at variance with the public good; and in every nation men are purposely trained from infancy to suppose that their well-being is incompatible with the progress and prosperity of other nations. Such are the means by which old society seeks to obtain the desired objects of life. The details now to be submitted have been devised upon principles which will lead to an opposite practice; to the combination of extensive mental and manual powers in the individuals of the working classes; to a complete identity of private and public interest; and to the training of nations to comprehend that their power and happiness cannot attain their full and natural development but through an equal increase of the power and happiness of all other states. These, therefore, are the real points at variance between that which *is* and that which *ought to be*.

It is upon these principles that arrangements are now proposed for the new agricultural villages, by which the food of the inhabitants may be prepared in one establishment, where they will eat together as one family.

By such arrangements the members of these new associations may be supplied with food at far less expense and with much more comfort than by any individual or family arrangements; and when the parties have been once trained and accustomed, as they easily may be, to the former mode, they will never afterwards feel any inclination to return to the latter.

If a saving in the quantity of food,—the obtaining of a superior quality of prepared provisions from the same materials,—and the operation of preparing them being effected in much less time, with far less fuel, and with greater ease, comfort, and health, to all the parties employed,—be advantages, these will be obtained in a remarkable manner by the new arrangements proposed.

When the new arrangements shall become familiar to the parties, this superior mode of living may be enjoyed at far less expense and with much less trouble than are necessary to procure such meals as the poor are now compelled to eat, surrounded by every object of discomfort and disgust, in the cellars and garrets of the most unhealthy courts, alleys, and lanes, in London,

Dublin, and Edinburgh, or Glasgow, Manchester, Leeds, and Birmingham.

Striking, however, as the contrast is in this description, and although the actual practice will far exceed what words can convey, yet there are many closet theorists and inexperienced persons, probably, who will still contend for individual arrangements and interests, in preference to that which they cannot comprehend.

These individuals must be left to be convinced by the facts themselves.

We now proceed to describe the interior accommodations of the private lodging-houses, which will occupy three sides of the parallelogram.

As it is of essential importance that there should be abundance of space within the line of the private dwellings, the parallelogram, in all cases, whether the association is intended to be near the maximum or the minimum in numbers, should be of large dimensions; and to accommodate a greater or less population, the private dwellings should be of one, two, three, or four stories, and the interior arrangements formed accordingly.

These will be very simple.

No kitchen will be necessary, as the public arrangements for cooking will supersede the necessity for any.

The apartments will be always well-ventilated, and, when necessary, heated or cooled on the improved principles lately introduced in the Derby Infirmary.[60]

To heat, cool, and ventilate their apartments, the parties will have no further trouble than to open or shut two slides, or valves, in each room, the atmosphere of which, by this simple contrivance, may always be kept temperate and pure.

One stove of proper dimensions, judiciously placed,

will supply the apartments of several dwellings with little trouble and at a very little expense, when the buildings are originally adapted for this arrangement.

Thus will all the inconveniences and expense of separate fires and fire-places, and their appendages, be avoided, as well as the trouble and disagreeable effects of mending fires and removing ashes, &c., &c.

Good sleeping apartments looking over the gardens in the country, and sitting-rooms of proper dimensions fronting the square, will afford as much lodging-accommodation, as, with the other public arrangements, can be useful to, or desired by, these associated cultivators.

Food and lodging being thus provided for, the next consideration regards dress.

Most persons take it for granted, without thinking on the subject, that to be warm and healthy it is necessary to cover the body with thick clothing[61] and to exclude the air as much as possible; and first appearances favour this conclusion. Facts, however, prove, that under the same circumstances, those who from infancy have been the most lightly clad, and who, by their form of dress, have been the most exposed to the atmosphere, are much stronger, more active, in better general health, warmer in cold weather, and far less incommoded by heat, than those who from constant habit have been dressed in such description of clothing as excludes the air from their bodies.

The Romans and the Highlanders[62] of Scotland appear to be the only two nations who adopted a national dress on account of its utility, without however neglecting to render it highly becoming and ornamental. The form of the dress of these nations was calculated first to give strength and manly beauty to the figure, and afterwards to display it to advantage. The time, expense, thought, and labour, now employed to create a variety of dress, the effects of which are to deteriorate the physical powers, and to render the human figure an object of pity and commiseration, are a certain proof of the low state of intellect among all classes in society.

All other circumstances remaining the same, sexual delicacy and virtue will be found much higher in nations among whom the person, from infancy, is the most exposed, than among those people who exclude from sight every part of the body except the eyes.

Although your Reporter is satisfied that the principle now stated is derived from the unchanging laws of nature, and is true to the utmost extent to which it can be carried; yet mankind must be trained in different habits, dispositions, and sentiments, before they can be permitted to act rationally on this, or almost any other law of nature.

The intermediate stage of society which your Reporter now recommends, admits, however, of judicious practical approximations towards the observance of these laws.

In the present case he recommends that the male children of the new villagers should be clothed in a dress somewhat resembling the Roman and Highland garb, in order that the limbs may be free from ligatures, and the air may circulate over every part of the body, and that they may be trained to become strong, active, well-limbed, and healthy.

And the females should have a well-chosen dress to secure similar important advantages.

The inhabitants of these villages, under the arrangements which your Reporter has in view, may be better dressed, for all the acknowledged purposes of dress, at much less than the one-hundredth part of the labour, inconvenience, and expense, that are now required to clothe the same number of persons in the middle ranks of life; while the form and material of the new dress will be acknowledged to be superior to any of the old.

Your Reporter has now to enter upon the most interesting portion of this division of the subject, and, he may add, the most important part of the economy of human life, with reference to the science of the influence of circumstances over the well-being and happiness of mankind, and to the full power and control which men may now acquire over those circumstances, and by which they may direct them to produce among the human race, with ease and certainty, either universal good or evil.

No one can mistake the application of these terms to the training and education of the children.

Since men began to think and write, much has been thought and written on this subject; and yet all that has been thought and written has failed to make the subject understood, or to disclose the principles on which we should proceed. Even now, the minds of the most enlightened are scarcely prepared to begin to think rationally respecting it. The circumstances of the times, however, require that a substantial advance should now be made in this part of the economy of human life.

Before any rational plan can be devised for the proper training and education of children, it should be distinctly known what capabilities and qualities infants and children possess, or, in fact, what they really are by nature.

If this knowledge is to be attained, as all human knowledge has been acquired, through the evidence of our senses, then it is evident that infants receive from a source and power over which they have no control, all the natural qualities they possess, and that from birth they are continually subjected to impressions derived from the circumstances around them; which impressions, combined with their natural qualities, (whatever fanciful speculative men may say to the contrary), do truly determine the character of the individual through every period of life.

The knowledge thus acquired will give to men the same kind of control over the combination of the natural powers and faculties of infants, as they now possess over the formation of animals: and although, from the nature of the subject, it must be slow in its progress and limited in extent, yet the time is not perhaps far distant when it may be applied to an important rational purpose, that is, to improve the breed of men, more than men have yet improved the breed of domestic animals.

But, whatever knowledge may be attained to enable man to improve the breed of his progeny at birth, facts exist in endless profusion to prove to every mind capable of reflection, that men may now possess a most extensive control over those circumstances which affect the infant after birth; and that, as far as such circumstances can influence the human character, the day has arrived when the existing generation may so far control them, that the rising generations may become in character, without any individual exceptions, whatever men can now desire them to be, that is not contrary to human nature.

Proceeding on these principles, your Reporter recommends arrangements by which the children shall be trained together as though they were literally all of one family.

For this purpose two schools will be required within the interior of the square, with spacious play and exercise grounds.

The schools may be conveniently placed in the line of buildings to be erected across the centre of the parallelograms, in connection with the church and places of worship.

The first School will be for the infants from two to six years of age. The second for children from six to twelve.

It may be stated, without fear of contradiction from any party who is master of the subject, that the whole success of these arrangements will depend upon the manner in which the infants and children shall be trained and educated in these schools. Men are, and ever will be, what they are and shall be made in infancy and childhood.

It is as evident as any fact can be made to man, that he does not possess the smallest control over the formation of any of his own faculties or powers, or over the peculiar and ever-varying manner in which those powers and faculties, physical and mental, are combined in each individual.

Such being the case, it follows that human nature up to this period has been misunderstood, vilified, and savagely ill-treated; and that, in consequence, the language and conduct of mankind respecting it form a compound of all that is inconsistent and incongruous and most injurious to themselves, from the greatest to the least.

It is upon these grounds that your Reporter, in educating the rising generation within his influence, ha long adopted principles different from those which ar usually acted upon.

He considers all children as beings whose dispositions, habits, and sentiments are to be formed *for* them; that these can be well-formed only by excluding all notions of reward, punishment, and emulation; and that, if their characters are not such as they ought to be, the error proceeds from their instructors and the other circumstances which surround them.

The children in these new schools should be therefore trained systematically to acquire useful knowledge through the means of sensible signs, by which their powers of reflection and judgment may be habituated to draw accurate conclusions from the facts presented to them. This mode of instruction is founded in nature, and will supersede the present defective and tiresome system of book learning, which is ill-calculated to give either pleasure or instruction to the minds of children. When arrangements founded on these principles shall be judiciously formed and applied to practice, children will, with ease and delight to themselves, acquire more real knowledge in a day, than they have yet attained under the old system in many months. They will not only thus acquire valuable knowledge, but the best habits and dispositions will be at the same time imperceptibly created in every one; and they will be trained to fill every office and to perform every duty that the well-being of their associates and the establishments can require. It is only by education, rightly understood, that communities of men can ever be well governed, and by means of such education every object of human society will be attained with the least labour and the most satisfaction.

It is obvious that training and education must be viewed as intimately connected with the employments of the association. The latter, indeed, will form an essential part of education under these arrangements. Each association, generally speaking, should create for itself a full supply of the usual necessaries, conveniences, and comforts of life.

The dwelling-houses and domestic arrangements being placed as near the centre of the land to be cultivated as circumstances will permit, it is concluded that the most convenient situation for the gardens will be adjoining the houses on the outside of the square; that these should be bounded by the principal roads; and that beyond them, at a sufficient distance to be covered by a plantation, should be placed the workshops and manufactory.

All will take their turn at some one or more of the occupations in this department, aided by every improvement that science can afford, alternately with employment in agriculture and gardening.

It has been a popular opinion to recommend a minute division of labour and a division of interests. It will presently appear, however, that this minute division of labour and division of interests are only other terms for poverty, ignorance, waste of every kind, universal opposition throughout society, crime, misery, and great bodily and mental imbecility.

To avoid these evils, which, while they continue, must keep mankind in a most degraded state, each child will receive a general education, early in life, that will fit him for the proper purposes of society, make him the most useful to it, and the most capable of enjoying it.

Before he is twelve years old he may with ease be trained to acquire a correct view of the outline of all the knowledge which men have yet attained.

By this means he will early learn what he is in relation

to past ages, to the period in which he lives, to the circumstances in which he is placed, to the individuals around him, and to future events. He will then only have any pretensions to the name of a rational being.

His physical powers may be equally enlarged, in a manner as beneficial to himself as to those around him. As his strength increases he will be initiated in the practice of all the leading operations of his community, by which his services, at all times and under all circumstances, will afford a great gain to society beyond the expense of his subsistence; while at the same time he will be in the continual possession of more substantial comforts and real enjoyments than have ever yet appertained to any class in society.

The new wealth which one individual, by comparatively light and always healthy employment, may create under the arrangements now proposed, is indeed incalculable. They would give him giant powers compared with those which the working class or any other now possesses. There would at once be an end of all mere animal machines, who could only follow a plough, or turn a sod, or make some insignificant part of some insignificant manufacture or frivolous article which society could better spare than possess. Instead of the unhealthy pointer of a pin,—header of a nail,—piecer of a thread—or clodhopper, senselessly gazing at the soil or around him, without understanding or rational reflection, there would spring up a working class full of activity and useful knowledge, with habits, information, manners, and dispositions, that would place the lowest in the scale many degrees above the best of any class which has yet been formed by the circumstances of past or present society.

Such are a few only of the advantages which a rational

mode of training and education, combined with the other parts of this system, would give to all the individuals within the action of its influence.

What, then, to sum up the whole in a few words, does your Reporter now propose to his fellow-creatures?

After a life spent in the investigation of the causes of the evils with which society is afflicted, and of the means of removing them,—and being now in possession of facts demonstrating the practicability and the efficacy of the arrangements now exhibited, which have been the fruit of that investigation, aided by a long course of actual experiments,—he offers to exchange their poverty for wealth, their ignorance for knowledge, their anger for kindness, their divisions for union. He offers to effect this change without subjecting a single individual even to temporary inconvenience.

His practical operations will commence with those who are now a burthen to the country for want of employment. He will enable these persons to support themselves and families, and pay the interest of the capital requisite to put their labour in activity. From the effects which will be thus produced on the character and circumstances of this oppressed class, the public will soon see and acknowledge that he has promised far less than will be realised; and when, by these arrangements, the vicious, the idle, and the pauper, shall be made virtuous, industrious, and independent, those who shall be still the lowest in the scale of old society may place themselves under the new arrangements, when they have evidence before them that these offer greater advantages than the old.

Upon this principle the change from the old system to the new will be checked in its progress whenever the latter ceases to afford decided inducements to embrace it; for long established habits and prejudices will continue to have a powerful influence over those who have been trained in them. The change, then, beyond the beneficial employment of those who now cannot obtain work, will proceed solely from proof, in practice, of the very great superiority of the new arrangements over the old. It calls for no sacrifice of principle or property to any individual in any rank or condition; through every step of its progress it effects unmixed good only.

Acting on principles merely approximating to those of the new system, and at the same time powerfully counteracted by innumerable errors of the old system, he has succeeded in giving to a population originally of the most wretched description, and placed under the most unfavourable circumstances, such habits, feelings, and dispositions, as enable them to enjoy more happiness than is to be found among any other population of the same extent in any part of the world; a degree of happiness, indeed, which it is utterly impossible for the old system to create among any class of persons placed under the most favourable circumstances.

Seeing, therefore, on the one hand, the sufferings which are now experienced, and the increasing discontent which prevails, especially among the most numerous and most useful class of our population, and, on the other, the relief and the extensive benefits which are offered to society on the authority of facts open to inspection,—can the public any longer with decency decline investigation? Can those who profess a sincere desire to improve the condition of the poor and working classes longer refuse to examine a proposal, which, on the most rational grounds, promises them ample relief, accompanied with unmixed good to every other part of society?

Your Reporter solicits no favour from any party; he belongs to none. He merely calls upon those who are the most competent to the task, honestly, as men valuing their own interests and the interests of society, to investigate, without favour or affection, a 'Plan (derived from thirty years' study and practical experience,) for relieving public distress and removing discontent, by giving permanent productive employment to the poor and working classes, under arrangements which will essentially improve their character and ameliorate their condition, diminish the expenses of production and consumption, and create markets co-extensive with production'.

# THE ADDRESS OF
# ROBERT OWEN

*At the Great Public Meeting, held at the National Equi-*
*table Labour Exchange, Charlotte-street, Fitzroy-square*
*[London], on the 1st of May, 1833, denouncing the Old*
*System of the World, and announcing the Commencement*
*of the New*

This Address, also published separately, appeared in
Owen's newspaper, *The Crisis*, 11 May 1833. An Editorial
described it as 'bold, uncompromising—the pure and undisguised language of truth...Such an address, in our
humble and independent views, makes a new era in freedom
of thought and liberty of expression. *It is the Magna Charta*
*of social regeneration.*' A report in the same issue described
the meeting, where Owen read the address 'to the thousands who were around him in the galleries, and below in the
open space, who listened to him with the most fixed attention,
and whose plaudits...were the most heartfelt and long-
continued we have ever witnessed'.

The existing condition of mankind makes it evident to
those who can reflect, and who have been formed with
minds capable of generalizing the ideas acquired from
the past and present history of the human race, that
the associations of men, from their commencement,
have been founded upon a false basis, and that, in
consequence, man has been found to be the creature of
error and deception, of sin and of misery.

   All associations have been based on the supposition
that man possesses the power to believe and to feel
according to the bidding of others; and that virtue consists in thus believing and feeling, and vice in refusing

so to believe and feel. And by analyzing the complex proceedings of mankind, it has been discovered that the system of forming the human character, and of governing the human race, derived from these notions, is the only system that has ever been known in any part of the world, and consequently is the only one that has yet been practised.

The experience of the past, the only valuable knowledge which man has acquired, proves that this system continually generates, and effectually cultivates, all the inferior animal passions—is opposed to the progress of real knowledge, to natural sincerity, to all the higher moral virtues, and to the finest and best feelings of our nature. Also, that as long as this system shall be supported, ignorance, poverty, and of necessity, sin and misery, must continually pervade all the associations of men; while pure charity and affection must remain as hitherto, unknown and unpractised.

Clearly perceiving this wretched state of human existence, and knowing that all governments are blind to its errors, inconsistencies, and wickedness, I have decided, after the most calm and deliberate reflection, to renounce on this day, thus publicly, in what may be justly called the metropolis of the civilized world, for myself and my disciples, the entire of this old system, and to declare my conviction that to countenance it any longer will be the grossest act of folly and the greatest of all crimes.

I also thus announce my determination henceforward to advocate thus openly and fairly another system, founded upon opposite principles, and leading to a totally different practice.

It is also my determination to recommend to all who think with me, to adopt the same course, and now to put these principles into full practice, and to assert the natural right of all men to act conscientiously, according to their convictions, as long as their conduct shall be beneficial to the public and not injurious to others.

If the existing laws of this country cannot protect the people in this moral and only really virtuous line of conduct, it is evident a despotism exists over the public mind which ought now to cease, and that the constitution of this and other countries ought to be changed to meet the improved intelligence of the age.

It is now the time to try the moral courage of men, and to ascertain who possesses virtue and knowledge sufficient to abandon falsehood for truth, folly for wisdom; yes, the period has arrived when the moral courage of man will be put to the test, and it will be proved who are prepared to overcome the mental bondage, in which, hitherto, all have been held from their infancy.

Do you feel desirous to ask me what we of the 'New World' now mean to relinquish, and what to adopt?

That none may misunderstand our proceedings, or falsify our intentions, I now thus openly, before the world, declare, that:— 1. We abandon all the false religions[63] that have been forced upon the human race, founded on the superstition that man, by his will, has the power to believe or feel as he likes, or to believe contrary to his convictions, or feel contrary to his nature, at the bidding of others.

2. We now adopt the only religion which can be true, because it is derived immediately from the unchangeable and everlasting laws of nature, which never lie, or deceive the human race. The basis of this Religion of Truth, the only one which ever can conduct man to the practice of pure charity and real virtue, and to the enjoy-

ment of unalloyed happiness, is the knowledge that the laws of nature have given the power to adult man, so to control the mental faculties and physical powers of his infant, as to force it to receive error, however absurd and inconsistent, or to imbibe truth only, known to be truth by its undeviating consistency with the ascertained laws of nature; and to acquire the most wretchedly vicious and injurious, or the most highly virtuous and beneficial habits through life: and thus, through our new religion, we attain the invaluable knowledge of the certain mode by which, without individual reward, or punishment, or responsibility, to make the whole human race morally, intellectually, and physically, either inferior or superior, good or bad, miserable or happy; and yet no two of them is likely ever to be formed to be without various desirable physical and mental differences.

3. Our future practice will be in conformity with this new religion, as far as the rapidly expiring errors of the old system shall be removed to admit its adoption, and the evils necessarily emanating from this old system we shall now adopt every means to make manifest to the human race.

4. We shall be opposed to no men, but solely to the old errors, which in the period of their mental weakness they have been compelled to receive.

5. In conformity with the principles of the new religion of demonstrable truth, we shall adore in admiring silence, as alone becomes man, that, to us at present, Incomprehensible Power, which acts in and through all nature, everlastingly composing, decomposing and recomposing the materials of the universe, producing the endless variety of life, of mind, and of organized form.

6. We will not degrade, blaspheme, or merely humanize this power, so far beyond man's present

knowledge as to attribute to it the human form and passions, or any of the qualities of our limited senses and vague imaginations.

7. Neither will we attempt to force others to receive or acknowledge our impressions upon this subject, seeing that up to this hour similar attempts have confounded and perplexed the human mind, making every man in every district of the world a degraded mental slave, irrational and miserable. On the contrary, we shall patiently wait until an evident accurate knowledge of this power shall be made manifest to all mankind, who will then, by the law of their nature, be compelled to admire and to love it, in proportion to the extent and the goodness of the qualities which it shall be discovered to possess.

By this course of proceeding, dictated by common sense, or plain right reasoning from self-evident facts, all injurious differences of opinions respecting religion will cease from among men; charity unlimited will take the place of presumption and violence; anger, ill-will, and irritation of all kinds will cease, and in place thereof pure love and affection, through a superior education, will be made to pervade and direct all the proceedings of mankind.

8. Directed by this knowledge and these feelings, we will, as soon as it shall be practicable, form arrangements to create New Institutions to new form the general character of the rising generation, and to regenerate the existing adult population; for the period is near at hand when the minds of men must be born again; when they shall no longer see as through a glass darkly, but face to face, and know each other even as they know themselves.

To effect this change, other arrangements, very different from those which now exist, will be formed to insure a superior education from birth, such as will give a new and very superior character to all children; arrangements that will preclude any child, free from mental disease or bodily defects, from acquiring physical, intellectual or moral injurious habits or qualities; and that will render the succeeding generations a superior order of beings compared with those who have hitherto lived.

9. As a knowledge of facts has now disclosed to us that, liking or disliking, or loving or hating, depend not upon the will of man, but upon the manner in which his organization is affected by the ever-varying qualities of external objects, none will be required to perjure themselves, as they are compelled to do under the old system of the world, before they can legally enjoy the natural rights of the sexes,[64] by solemnly declaring that they will love to the end of life a being who is liable to perpetual change, and whom they may be forced to dislike or hate before the year expires. No! instead of this blasphemy against the laws of nature, other arrangements dictated by common sense, or right reason, will be formed to insure all the good that can be derived, and to avoid all the vice and evil that has been experienced from the social converse between the sexes. All will then be fully conscious, and will openly acknowledge, that pure chastity consists in forming this connexion only when affection exists between the parties, and that it is a vile, abominable, and injurious prostitution to form or continue this connexion when there is no affection between the parties, even when they are what is called legally bound to each other. The union between the sexes will be, in consequence, always pure and chaste; it will be a union of affection

only—it will continue as long as that affection can be maintained, and cease only, under well-devised public forms and regulations, when the affection between the parties can no longer be made to exist. And the experience of the world has proved that affection is more disinterested, pure, and durable, without than with these legal bonds. In order to prevent confusion or any evil whatever by these changes, other arrangements, very different from the existing family arrangements, will be made, in conformity with this superior union between the sexes, and the superior national education to be provided for the children.

10. We shall abandon the present degrading and demoralizing mode of distributing wealth by the ordinary method in practice, of buying cheap and selling dear, through the medium of the common money of the old system of the world. Arrangements will be made, as speedily as possible, to effect an equitable exchange of labour for equal value of labour throughout society, by the intervention of the *labour note*,[65] the most perfect money in all respects ever yet introduced into society. But this method of transacting the business of life will be an intermediate and temporary arrangement only, and will be continued no longer than till permanent arrangements can be formed to re-constitute society upon the scientific principles, giving to each separate division of society, in practice, the due proportion of the producing, distributing, educating, and governing principles, so combined and organized that more of all kinds of wealth, possessing intrinsic value, may be, with advantage to all parties, so easily created, that those made to be the most penurious or avaricious will cease to desire any individual accumulation of it; and all contests, private or public, for the possession

of wealth will terminate for ever. And then all the human powers and faculties will be directed, to promote in a straightforward manner, to the exclusion of all private interests, the general happiness of the whole of society.

11. Conscious of the unlimited powers possessed by the British nation when wisely united in its operations, to produce wealth through all future time, far beyond the wants or desires of its population, we renounce the principle of individual competition in the production and distribution of wealth, as being, in its immediate and remote consequences, not only the most demoralizing principle on which man can now act and govern his affairs, but as being, also, the greatest obstacle, in practice, to the beneficial production and distribution of wealth, to the formation of a superior individual and national character, and to the well-ordering and good government of the people.

We shall, therefore, as soon as the means can be obtained, exchange the principle of competition, and of mistaken individual interest, for the principle of unlimited union and of undivided national interests. And by this change in conducting the affairs of this empire, we know that more and better wealth can be produced in one day than is now produced in one week; that this greater amount and better quality of wealth can be more advantageously distributed for the whole population, by one day's occupation of those at present employed to distribute wealth, than is now effected by them under the existing competitive system of distribution in one month: that by this change, with less labour and capital than are now applied to the task the individual and national character can be formed to be many hundred-fold superior to that which has been, is, or can be found under the competition system, and that by the abandonment of the principle of division of interests, the empire will be more easily and far better governed than it ever has been under the old system, with one per cent. of the capital and labour which are now required.

13. As the false basis upon which the moral part of the old system has been founded, united with the principle of competition, when applied to practice, form together the sole cause which renders law, or codes of law, necessary in society, we, of the new world, renounce all law proceedings in our transactions with each other, and we will form arrangements to adjust whatever differences may arise between individuals, or associations of individuals, by the decision of three persons selected for their superior knowledge and experience in the new principles, and their known love of justice; these individuals to be annually chosen by the elders of their district.

Courts of law, and all the paraphernalia and folly of law, with its animosities and ruinous expense, cannot be found in a rational state of society and will, therefore, not be found among the children of the new world.

14. As the principles on which this new system is based will immediately check, and effectually prevent the growth of anger and ill will, and speedily remove all the causes of dislike from among the children trained from infancy in the new world, war will be discountenanced, and ultimately abrogated as a practice, the most grossly ignorant and vicious that a well ordered or rational mind can conceive; a practice contrary to our new religion, and to be followed only by those who have been made irrational from their birth or by wholesale murderers and robbers.

Charity, peace, and good-will to the whole family of mankind, without regard to any of the petty artificial or irrational causes of division now existing between them, will be the inevitable, and, therefore, uniform practice of all the children of the new world; and one of their chief offices, until the ignorance which causes the evil shall be removed, will be to reconcile man to man, and nation to nation, throughout the world, and to enable all to understand that they have but one interest, which is, to insure the permanent happiness of each and all, to promote which, by every means that the aggregate of knowledge and power can devise, will be the great business of human life, and then will be seen how easy and straightforward is the true path to real virtue and the most refined enjoyments.

15. But although the private and public warfare and contests, with their endless train of unavoidable crime and misery, will be unknown among the children of the new world, effeminacy, with its train of evil, will also be discountenanced and discarded. The new mode of forming the character of the children of the new world will cultivate, and bring forth to maturity and perfection, all the physical, intellectual, and moral faculties and powers which have been given to human nature. Arrangements will be formed to admit and encourage the due exercise of each of these faculties and powers up to the point of temperance, for it is only by all of them being called into action at the period designed by nature, that man can feel satisfied, contented, and happy. Anxiety is the natural feeling which arises when any one of these propensities or qualities is not duly exercised. The physical powers will, therefore, be better cultivated than they were in the best days of Greece and Rome, and a far superior form of body and

expression of mind, and a duly regulated activity of both will be obtained for all the future generations.

In consequence, celibacy, in either sex, beyond the period designed by nature, will no longer be considered a virtue, but, on the contrary, it will be known to be, as it is, a great crime against nature, causing other un-natural crimes, all of which produces disease of body and mind, giving a false direction to both thoughts and feelings, and thereby making the human race the most artificial, unnatural and criminal beings in existence. The earth is yet a wilderness for want of people[66] to drain its marshes and cultivate its soil, nor does it yet produce one thousandth part of the excellence and enjoyment which it is capable of bringing forth and permanently sustaining. Upon this, and almost all other important subjects, the world is in gross darkness, because it has hitherto been instructed and governed, or rather uninstructed and misgoverned, by men trained to possess only the most feeble and puny knowledge of themselves, of nature, and of wise and good government.

16. We now also renounce the separate interests which have been created by the errors of the old world; and we will adopt another mode of carrying on the general business of society. Originally many and various occupations were performed by one individual; but as population increased in particular places, the variety of employments practised by one person gradu-ally diminished, until they are now become so much divided, that many individuals have their time and attention taken up and occupied in making a small part of a common pin,[67] a needle, or of thread, to the de-struction of their health, their mental faculties, and all the higher enjoyments of a rational existence. Ex-perience has now developed the means by which the

union and division of labour may be combined to secure
the peculiar advantages of both, without the evils of
either. The science of society, so totally unknown in the
old world, has disclosed the necessity for, and the
benefits of, uniting a due proportion of agriculture,
manufactures, commerce, education, and government,
in every separate association, for carrying on the business of life; and in the new world all these individualised
and opposing interests will become one, and each part
thus united, will essentially aid and promote all the
others. The communities of the new world, when the
public shall acquire any rational notions respecting
them, will be found to be nothing less than a combination of all these interests, so united as to insure to every
individual living within them, the greatest amount of
advantages, and the highest degree of individual freedom and happiness that human nature, in its present
state of knowledge, is capable of enjoying. Thus will
man, as a member of an association formed purposely
for his benefit, experience the utmost share of individual freedom that is compatible with the still higher
privileges of a social state of existence.

17. We consequently abandon all the arrangements
to which these separate interests have given birth; such
as large cities,[68] towns, villages, and universities,[69] as
well as the existing arrangements for carrying on the
business of agriculture, detached from manufactures,
education, and commerce. These accidental individual
circumstances, formed without knowledge or foresight,
are not such as can ever form man into a rational
being, or insure to him more than a very small portion
of the wealth, health, and happiness, which his nature
may be made to enjoy.

18. We also abandon, to the irrationality of the old

system of the world, all places for ceremonial worship of an unknown Power, and with them all mysteries in every department of life, as being much worse than useless. In like manner, we abandon to the same system all places of punishment and confinement, such as Prisons, Penitentiaries, Houses of Correction, and Workhouses; and all charitable institutions, as they are called, as being prominent and magnificent monuments of the utter incapacity of the rulers of human affairs, to form arrangements to insure a superior character, wealth, and health of body and mind, to the respective populations which they have governed or do now attempt to govern.

19. We abandon also all individual ambition, and desire for personal distinction, knowing we possess nothing but what we have received, and that these personal distinctions cannot benefit mankind but are, in themselves, the cause of endless errors, crimes, and miseries, and tend to keep men in perpetual ignorance of themselves, and to make them highly irrational.

20. We also dismiss, for similar reasons, all envy and jealousy from the new world, in which all will partake of the advantages derived from the excellencies of each; all will, therefore, feel their happiness to be increased in proportion as each excels in all superior qualifications, and in consequence all will aid to enable each individual to acquire and enjoy them. Thus will unity of design, of duty, of interest, and of sympathy, among the human race, supersede the division, competition, and opposition of man to man, and nation to nation, and remove the causes of all the envy and jealousy which instigate to crime, make man a demon, and the earth a pandemonium.

I therefore now proclaim to the world the commencement, on this day, of the promised millenium, founded on rational principles and consistent practice.

# [ONE OF] SIX LECTURES

*delivered in Manchester previously
to the Discussion between Mr. Robert Owen
and the Rev. J. H. Roebuck*

These extracts are from Lecture v, 'The natural and rational classification of society'. The lectures as a whole, delivered in 1837, illustrate Owen's emphasis from the late thirties on a socialist concern with rights, including those to leisure and happiness, and his programme for an ideal world.

As all men are born ignorant and inexperienced, and must receive their knowledge, either from the instincts of their nature, which are given to them at their birth, or from surrounding external objects, animate and inanimate, which they do not create; all, by nature have equal rights.

The distinctions of class and station, are artificial, and have been conceived and adopted by men, while they were ignorant, inexperienced, and irrational. It is now proposed to supersede them, by the natural and rational divisions into which, experience will prove, it will be greatly for the interest and happiness of all, that society should now resolve itself.

No man has a right to require another man to do for him, what he will not do for that man; or, in other words, all men, by nature, have equal rights.

The natural and rational classification, when adopted, will for ever preserve those rights inviolate, and it is, beyond all estimate, for the interest or happiness of the human race, that this classification should be now universally adopted, for it would immediately calm the evil passions, terminate every contest, private and public, individual and national, and introduce order and wisdom into all the affairs of mankind.

The progress made in a knowledge of various sciences, giving man, by a right direction of it, the power over the production of wealth and the formation of character, now renders the change, from the irrational to the rational classification, an act of necessity.

The natural and rational classification of the human race is, then, the classification of age—each division of age having the occupations to perform, for which, each age is the best adapted by nature.

There will be no occupation requisite to be performed by one which will not be equally performed by all, and by all, far more willingly than any of the general affairs of life are now performed, by any class, from the sovereign to the pauper.

In the present irrational state of the human mind and human affairs, no one can form a true conception of what individuals may be trained and educated to acquire and accomplish, at their various periods of life.

Because it is yet unknown what are the capabilities of human nature, when it shall not be forced to imbibe error and falsehood from its birth; when it shall not be daily trained in most injurious habits, and artificial manners; when it shall be taught truth, only, by every word, look, and action of all around it, when it shall be educated to acquire the best habits for its own happiness, and the well-being of society; when it shall attain the individual self sustaining manners which, by such training, will naturally arise and insure pleasure, by its variety, to all; when it shall possess the valuable knowledge which by such training and education will be given to it, and when it shall acquire the facilities in the practice of the operations of society, in which, as it advances in life, it will be instructed.

It is somewhat difficult, previously to additional experience, to decide very accurately what should be the precise permanent divisions of human life[70] to form the best classification. But there is now, sufficient knowledge for present purposes, and experience will afford more, as soon as it shall be required.

Probably, periods of five years, up to thirty, will afford a present useful classification, and each class to be occupied as follows.

First class or from birth to the end of the fifth year.

To be so placed, trained, and educated as that they may be in a proper temperature for their age, fed with the most wholesome food; lightly and loosely clothed; regularly duly exercised in a pure atmosphere; also that their dispositions may be formed to have their greatest pleasure in attending to, and promoting the happiness of all who may be around them; that they may acquire an accurate knowledge, as far as their young capacities will easily admit, of the objects which they can see and handle, and that no false impression be made on any of their senses by those around them refusing a simple explanation to any of their questions; that they may have no knowledge of individual punishment or reward, or be discouraged from always freely expressing their thoughts and feelings; that they may be taught as early as their minds can receive it, that the thoughts and feelings of others, are, like their own, instincts of human nature which they are compelled to have, and thus, to acquire in infancy the rudiments of charity and affection for all; that they may have no fear of, but full and implicit confidence in every one around them, and that the universal selfish, or individual feeling, of our animal existence, may be so directed as to derive its chief gratification from contributing to the pleasure and happiness of others.

By these measures, a solid foundation will be laid for sound minds, good habits, superior natural manners, fine dispositions and some useful knowledge. By these means they will be so well prepared before they leave this class, that, for their age, they will think, speak and act rationally. They will be, therefore, at the end of this period, in many respects, in advance of the average of human beings, as they are now taught and placed, at any time of their lives.

The first class being prepared by this new rational nursing and infant training, will leave the nursing and infant school to be removed into the appropriate arrangements for the second class; which class will consist of children from five to ten years complete.

This class will be lodged, fed and clothed upon the same general principles as the first class, making only the difference which their age requires; but, now, their exercises will consist in that which will be permanently useful. According to their strength and capacities they will acquire a practice in some of the lighter operations of the business of life; operations, which may be easily made to afford them far more pleasure and gratification than can be derived from the useless toys of the old world. Their knowledge will be now chiefly acquired from personal inspection of objects, and familiar conversation with those more experienced than themselves. By this plan, being judiciously pursued, under rational arrangements properly adapted for the purpose, these children will, in two years, become willing, intelligent assistants in the domestic arrangements and gardens for some hours in the day, according to their strength.

Continuing this mode of education, these children from seven to ten will become efficient operators in whatever their physical strength will enable them easily to accomplish, and whatever they do, they will perform as a matter of amusement, and for exercise, with their equally intelligent and delightful companions. These exercises they will pursue under the immediate directions of the juniors of the third class.

At ten, they will be well trained rational beings; superior in mind, manner, dispositions, feelings, and conduct to any who have yet lived, and their deficiency in physical strength, will be amply supplied, by the superior mechanical and chemical powers which will be contrived and arranged, to be ready for them to direct when they enter the next class. These new operations will be, to them, a continual source of instruction and amusement, and to which they will look forward with the delight experienced by the acquisition of new important attainments.

The members of the second class, when they shall complete their tenth year, will enter the third class, which will consist of those from ten to fifteen years complete. This class will be engaged, the first two years, that is, from ten to twelve, in directing and assisting those in the second class from seven to ten, in their domestic exercises in the house, gardens, and pleasure grounds; and from twelve to fifteen, they will be engaged in acquiring a knowledge of the principles and practices of the more advanced useful arts of life; a knowledge by which they will be enabled to assist in producing, the greatest amount, of the most valuable wealth, in the shortest time, with the most pleasure to themselves and advantage to society. This will include all the productions required from the soil; from mines; from fisheries; the arts of manufacturing food, to keep and to prepare it, in the best manner, for daily use; the art of working up the materials to prepare them for garments, buildings, furniture, machinery, instruments, and implements for all purposes, and to produce, prepare and execute, whatever society requires, in the best manner that the concentrated wisdom and capital of society can direct. In all these operations the members of this class, from twelve to fifteen years, will daily assist, for as many hours as will not injure their physical strength, mental powers or moral feelings, and with their previous training, with the daily superior instruction and aid which they will receive from the members of the class immediately above them; they will perform all that will be necessary for them to do, with no more exercise than their physical and mental health will require to keep them in the best state of body and mind. In these five years, also, they will make a great advance in the knowledge of all the sciences; for they will be surrounded with every facility to acquire accurately the most valuable knowledge in the shortest time.

They will now be well prepared to enter the fourth class, which will be formed of those from fifteen to twenty years complete. This class will enter upon a most interesting period of human life; within its duration, its members will become men and women of a new race, physically, intellectually, and morally; beings far superior to any yet known to have lived upon the earth—their thoughts and feelings will have been formed in public, without secresy of any kind; for as they passed through the previous divisions, they would naturally make known to each other, in all simplicity, their undisguised thoughts and feelings.

Each one will be, thus, well educated, physically,

intellectually, and morally. Under this classification and consequent arrangement of these associated families, wealth unrestrained in its production by any of the artificial absurdities now so common in all countries, will be most easily produced in superfluity; all will be secured in a full supply of the best of it, for all purposes that may be required. They will, therefore, all be equal in their education and condition, and no artificial distinction, or any distinction but that of age, will ever be known among them.

There will be then, no motive or inducement for any parties to unite, except from pure affection arising from the most unreserved knowledge of each others character, in all respects, as far as it can be known before the union takes place. There will be no artificial obstacles in the way of the permanent happy union of the sexes, for under the arrangements of this new state of human existence, the affections will receive every aid which can be devised to induce them to be permanent; and under these arrangements, there can be no doubt, that, as the parties will be placed as far as possible in the condition of lovers during their lives, the affections will be far more durable, and produce far more pleasure and enjoyment to the parties, and far less injury to society, than has ever yet been experienced, under any of the varied arrangements which have emanated from the imagined free-will agency of the human race.

If, however, these superior arrangements to produce happiness between the sexes, should fail in some partial instances, which it is possible may yet occur, measures will be introduced by which, without any severance of friendship, between the parties, a separation may be made, the least injurious to them and the most beneficial to the interests of society.

No immorality can exceed that which is sure to arise from society compelling individuals to live continually together, when they have been made, by the laws of their nature, to lose their affections for each other, and to entertain them for another object. How much dreadful misery has been inflicted upon the human race through all past ages, from this single error? How much demoralization! How many murders! How much secret unspeakable suffering, especially, to the female sex! How many evils are experienced over the world, at this moment, arising from this single error of the imaginary free-will system by which men have been so long, so ignorantly and miserably governed!

This fourth class will be still more active and general producers of the various kinds of wealth required by society, as well as the kind and intelligent instructors of the senior members of the third class.

It is not improbable, that these four classes, under such simplified arrangements in all the departments of life, as may now be made, will be sufficient to produce a surplus of all the wealth, which a rational and superior race of beings can require; but to remove all doubt respecting this part of the subject, and to make the business of life a pleasure to all, another class of producers of wealth, and instructors in knowledge, shall be added, and they will form the fifth class; which class will consist of those from 20 to 25 years complete.

This will form the highest and most experienced class of producers and instructors, and beyond the age of this class, none need be required to produce or instruct, except for their own pleasure and gratification. This fifth class will be the superiors and directors in each branch of production and of education. They will perform in a very superior manner, that which is now most defectively done by the principal proprietors and active directing partners of large producing establishments; and by the Professors of Universities.

The great business of human life is, first, to produce abundance of the most valuable wealth for the use and enjoyment of all; and secondly, to educate all to well use and properly enjoy their wealth after it has been produced.

The sixth class will consist of those from twenty-five to thirty years of age complete.

The business of this will be to preserve the wealth produced by the previous classes in order that no waste may arise, that all kinds of it may be kept in the best condition, and used, when in the most perfect state, for the beneficial enjoyment of all parties. They will also have to direct the distribution of it, as it may be required from the stores, for the daily use of the family. Under the arrangements which may be, and no doubt will be formed for these purposes, two hours each day will be more than sufficient to execute the regular business of this class, in a very superior manner. Some part of the remainder of the day they will most likely feel the greatest pleasure in occupying with visits to various parts of their beautiful and interesting establishment, to see how every process is advancing, with each of which, by their previous training they will be familiar, and now, at their leisure, they may consider whether any improvement can be made in them for the general benefit. Another portion of the day they will probably devote to their most favorite studies, whether in the fine arts, in the sciences, in trying experiments, in reading, or conversation, or in making excursions to the neighbouring establishments, to give or to receive information, or to make visits of friendship.

This would be the prime period for the more active enjoyments of life, and all would be, by this classification, most amply enabled to enjoy them. They would have high health, physical and mental; they would have a constant flow of good spirits; they would by this period, have secured a greater breadth and depth of the most varied useful knowledge in principle and practice, than any human beings have ever yet attained; they would, also, be familiar with those acquirements which, in addition to their attainments in that which is useful in principle and practice, would render them delightful companions to each other, and to all with whom they may come into communication. And they would be, thus, preparing themselves to become fit members of the class immediately in advance of them, that is, the seventh class. This will consist of all the members of the family, from thirty to forty years inclusive.

The business of this class will be to govern the home department, in such manner as to preserve the establishment in peace, charity and affection; or, in other words, to prevent the existence of any causes which may disturb the harmony of the proceedings. And this result will be most easily effected for the following reasons.—First, because they will know what their own nature really is, and that, the convictions and feelings of the individuals are not created by their will, but that they are instincts of their nature which they must possess and retain, until some new motive or cause shall effect a change in them.—Secondly, because, in consequence of this knowledge, all, in the establishment, will be rational in their thoughts, feelings, and conduct; there will, therefore, be no anger, ill-will, bad temper, inferior or evil passions, uncharitableness, or unkindness. —Thirdly, because no one will find fault with another for his physical, intellectual, or moral nature, or acquired character; as all will know how these have been formed; but all will, of necessity, feel a deep interest in doing whatever may be in their power, by kindness directed by judgment, to improve these qualities in every individual.

Fourthly, because there will be no poverty, or fear of poverty, or want of any kind.

Fifthly, because there will be no disagreeable objects within or around the establishment to annoy, or to produce an injurious or unpleasant effect upon any one.

Sixthly, because, according to age, there would be a perfect equality in their education, condition, occupations, and enjoyments.

Seventhly, because by their training, mode of life, and the superior arrangements, in accordance with, and congenial to their nature, and by which they would be continually influenced and governed, they would, very generally, if not always, enjoy sound health and good spirits.

Eighthly, because there would be no motive to engender ambition, jealousy, or revenge.

Ninthly, because there would be no secresy or hypocrisy of any kind.

Tenthly, because there would be no buying or selling for a monied profit.

Eleventhly, because there could be no money, the cause now of so much oppression and injustice.

Twelfthly, because there would be no religious or injurious mental perplexities or estranged feelings, on account of religious or other differences of opinion.

Thirteenthly, because there would be no pecuniary anxieties, for wealth of superior qualities would everywhere superabound.

Fourteenthly, because there would be no disappointment of the affections; both sexes rationally and naturally enjoying the rights of their nature, at the period designed by nature and most beneficially to insure to all virtue and happiness.

Fifteenthly, and lastly, because, every one would know that permanent arrangements had been purposely devised and executed to ensure impartial justice to every one, by each being, so placed, trained and educated from birth to maturity, that he would be, as he advanced in age, secure of experiencing all the advantages and enjoyments which the accumulated wisdom of his predecessors knew how to give to the faculties and powers which he derived from nature.

This class of domestic governors would, naturally, for order and convenience, divide themselves into sub-committees, each of which sub-committees, would, more immediately, superintend or govern some one of the departments which would be divided between them, in the best manner their experience would direct.

By these arrangements and classifications every one would know, at an early age, that at the proper period of life, he would have, without contest, his fair full share of the government of society.

But final decision upon every doubtful point of practice must rest somewhere; and it is, perhaps, most natural, that this power should be vested in the oldest member of this class who will possess this precedence for one year only, because, at the termination of that period, he will be superseded by the next senior member of this class, and he will become a junior member of the eighth class, which will consist of those from forty to sixty years complete.

After providing for the production of wealth, for its

preservation and distribution; for the training, education and formation of character from birth to maturity, and for the internal government of each establishment; it is necessary to make arrangements, to connect each establishment with all other establishments founded on the same principles, or to form what may not be improperly called the external and foreign arrangements.

The eighth class will have charge of this department; a department so important to place under the direction of the best informed and most experienced yet active members of society. The individuals from forty to sixty years of age will be so informed and experienced as a class, after they shall have regularly passed through the seven previous classes.

Their business will be to receive and attend to visitors from other establishments; to correspond with other establishments; to visit, and to arrange the general business of public roads, conveyances and exchanges of surplus produce, inventions, improvements and discoveries, in order, that the population, of every district, should freely partake of the benefits to be derived from the concentrated knowledge and acquirements of the world, and that no part should remain in an ignorant or barbarous state.

This period of human life will be one of high utility and enjoyment. For the earth will not be the wild barren waste, swamp or forest, which, with some exceptions, it ever has been and yet is; the united efforts of a well trained world, will speedily change it into a well drained, highly cultivated, and beautiful pleasure scene, which, by its endless variety, will afford health and enjoyment to all, to a degree, such as the human mind in its present degraded and confined state, has not the capacity to imagine.

# NOTES

## THE LIFE OF ROBERT OWEN

**1.** p. 42, **Stamford.** He served a three-year apprentice-ship with Mr James McGuffog, who had a business 'for the sale of the best and finest articles of female wear'. At fourteen he left for London, where he worked for Messrs Flint and Palmer, drapers, 'an old-established house on old London Bridge, Boroughside' (*Life*, pp. 17, 25).

**2.** p. 44, **About this period.** Owen had come to Manchester about 1786–8 to work for Mr Satterfield ('His establishment was then the first in his line in the retail department,' *Life*, p. 29). In 1791 Owen set up in partner-ship, on £100 capital borrowed from his brother, with a Mr Jones, manufacturing machines for spinning fine cotton. The partnership had been dissolved and Owen was now in business on his own.

**3.** p. 48, **Dr. Percival.** Dr Thomas Percival, Manchester physician, educated at Warrington Academy, familiar with many famous eighteenth-century European thinkers. His 'Heads of Resolutions' for the Manchester Board of Health (which he was instrumental in establishing, and of which Owen was a member), is a well-known document in early factory reform. He established the Manchester Literary and Philosophical Society in 1781.

**4.** p. 48, **'Manchester College'.** Manchester Academy, founded in 1786 after the closing of Warrington Academy, to continue the Unitarian tradition. It eventually became Manchester College, Oxford, a training college for Unitarian ministers. See J. W. A. Smith, *The Birth of Modern Education* (1954), pp. 160–71, for a description of Warrington and Manchester Academies. 'Baines' is a mistake for 'Barnes'.

**5.** p. 48, **John Dalton.** Taught mathematics and natural philosophy at the Manchester Academy from 1793. He was active in the Manchester Literary and Philosophical Society for half a century, became its president, and published many of his scientific papers in the *Memoirs* of the Society.

**6.** p. 48, **Coleridge.** There is no corroborative evidence for this encounter between Owen and the poet, though it is known that Coleridge did visit Manchester.

**7.** p. 49, **I had now to commence.** Owen had visited Glasgow and seen the New Lanark cotton mills. Learning that David Dale, the proprietor, who had founded the mills with Richard Arkwright in 1784, might be interested in selling them, Owen approached Dale. Owen and his partners in the Chorlton Twist Co. bought the mills at a price which Dale asked Owen to name. Owen took over direction of the New Lanark mills 'about the first of January 1800'.

**8.** p. 56, **Lancaster.** Owen was attracted by Joseph Lancaster's efforts, through an undenominational monitorial scheme, to spread elementary education, though he recognised the limitations of Lancaster's system. A committee was formed in 1808 to organise Lancaster's affairs, and set up a Lancasterian Society, which took the title of British and Foreign School Society in 1814.

**9.** p. 56, **Dr. Bell.** The National Society for Promoting the Education of the Poor in the Principles of the Established Church was established in 1811. There is additional testimony to this support by Owen in Robert Dale Owen's autobiography, *Threading My Way*.

**10.** p. 58, **For the second time.** See note 7 above.

**11.** p. 58, **I went to London.** Owen had met with obstruction from a second set of partners to his plans, particularly for the schools. He had written the first essay of *A New View of Society* in 1812.

**12.** p. 59, **Such partners.** All of them, except Michael Gibbs, were nonconformists. Fox, Allen and Foster were all members of the committee formed in 1808 to save Lancaster from financial ruin. Only William Allen, eminent partner in the drug firm of Allen and Hanbury, took an active interest in New Lanark, his Quaker beliefs bringing him into conflict with Owen, and eventually contributing to Owen's withdrawal from New Lanark. For Allen, Fox and the Lancasterian movement see David Salmon, *William Allen*, reprinted from the *Educational Record* (1905).

**13.** p. 59, **Leading men of that period.** This is no idle list. Owen in this period did indeed visit, appear on public platforms, sit on committees and correspond with leading public figures of every kind.

**14.** p. 61, **My opening speech.** See also p. 16 above.

**15.** p. 61, **Heads of both.** Owen describes visits to the Prime Minister, Lord Liverpool, to the Home Secretary, Lord Sidmouth, and to the Archbishop of Canterbury, and cordial receptions by all of them.

**16.** p. 64, **James Buchanan.** Owen was disparaging about Buchanan's abilities after he left New Lanark to become the master at the first infant school in London, at Brewers Green, Westminster, in 1819. For a defence of Buchanan, and a discussion of the possibility that he played a larger part at New Lanark than Owen describes, see R. R. Rusk, *A History of Infant Education*, 1951 (2nd edition), pp. 135–45.

**17.** p. 65, **Unsuccessful attempts.** None of the infant schools of the 1820s and 1830s associated with the Mayos and Samuel Wilderspin, for example, did in fact reach (or even aim for) the standard of generous kindness and understanding of children demonstrated at New Lanark.

**18.** p. 65, **Lord Brougham.** Henry Brougham, Whig politician, utilitarian, Edinburgh Reviewer and educational reformer. The history of parliamentary efforts to provide education for the people 'between 1816, when he moved for the first Select Committee, up to 1839, when the Committee of Council was appointed, is mainly a record of efforts, in which he took a prominent and distinguished part' (Francis Adams, *History of the Elementary School Contest in England*, 1882, p. 67). Brougham figures frequently in the story of Owen's life.

## A NEW VIEW OF SOCIETY

**19.** p. 74, **Late Ruler of France.** Owen maintained that a copy of *A New View of Society* reached Napoleon on Elba. Owen makes the far-fetched suggestion that 'Buonaparte had read and studied this work with great attention, and had determined on his return to power, if the Sovereigns of Europe had allowed him to remain quietly on the throne of France, to do as much for peace and progress, as he had previously done for war...But they knew not, and did not believe, that he had changed his views...' (*Life*, p. 155).

**20.** p. 76, **Without domestic revolution.** Owen always argued against revolution, precipitate political action, and even action for parliamentary reform. His argument constantly was that social change needed to be rationally planned and executed, and political action was either unreliable or irrelevant. In this he clashed both with the utilitarians and with the working-class radicals (and did not identify himself with the Chartists). See also note 32 below.

**21.** p. 83, **St. Giles's.** This district of London was a nineteenth-century symbol of urban anarchy and degradation. In 1844 Engels found that the district, close to the fashionable streets of the West End, 'beggars all description. There is hardly an unbroken windowpane...The doors, where they exist, are made of old boards nailed together. Indeed in this nest of thieves doors are superfluous, because there is nothing worth stealing...Here live the poorest of the poor' (*The Condition of the Working Class in England*, trans. Henderson and Chaloner, 1958, p. 34). For an even more harrowing picture see Charles Kingsley's novel *Alton Locke*, chapter VIII.

**22.** p. 85, **Mr. Dale.** See p. 24 and note 7 above.

**23.** p. 85, **Cotton mills were first introduced.** Arkwright's water-frame, patented in 1769, was powered by water and later steam, and 'was a factory machine from the beginning...This was the real beginning of the departure from domestic industry' (Deane, *The First Industrial Revolution*, p. 87).

**24.** p. 88. **The ages of six, seven, and eight.** Young children worked, of course, in domestic occupations before the industrial revolution, but the early years of the cotton industry saw the wholesale, unregulated apprenticeship of pauper children to the mills. 'Wagon loads of children were taken from the London streets and apprenticed to manufacturers in Lancashire. In defiance or in evasion of the law, they often began to work at the ages of five or six' (Adams, *History of the Elementary School Contest*, p. 5).

**25.** p. 89, **Some English merchants and manufacturers.** Owen and his partners. The essays were originally published anonymously, by 'One of his Majesty's Justices of Peace for the County of Lanark'.

**26.** p. 94, **The support fund.** 'This fund arose from each individual contributing one sixtieth part of their wages, which, under their own management, was applied to support the sick, the injured by accident, and the aged' (Owen's note).

**27.** p. 94, **Apprentices.** See note 24 above.

**28.** p. 94, **Ten years old.** 'It may be remarked, that even this age is too early to keep them at constant employment in manufactories from six in the morning to seven in the evening. Far better would it be for the children, their parents, and for society, that the first should not commence employment until they attain the age of twelve, when their education might be finished, and their bodies would be more competent to undergo the fatigue and exertions required of them. When parents can be trained to afford this additional time to their children without inconvenience, they will, of course, adopt the practice now recommended' (Owen's note).

**29.** p. 94, **In process of adoption.** 'To avoid the inconveniences which must ever arise from the introduction of a particular creed into a school, the children are taught to read in such books as inculcate those precepts of the

Christian religion which are common to all denominations'
(Owen's note).

**30.** p. 95, **Covering the original expense.** Owen's
store sold good-quality food and clothing cheaply. 'The
prices charged, though...some 25 per cent. lower than those
of the private shopkeepers, were yet sufficient to cover all
the expenses of the business, and leave a profit of about
£700 a year, which was devoted entirely to the maintenance
of the schools' (Podmore, *Robert Owen*, 1923 edition, p. 86).
Podmore suggests that Owen may have 'improved and set
going again a store already started by Dale'.

**31.** p. 98, **Such flagrant injustice.** Owen believed
throughout his life that prince, parliament and church were
amenable ultimately to reasonable persuasion and would
not, if true principles were adequately and persistently explained to them, act unjustly.

**32.** p. 98, **One measure called a reform.** Owen and
the radical reformers were to clash publicly at a series of
meetings organised in London by Owen in 1817. Owen
showed no interest in the tradition of parliamentary reform
agitation from the Society for Constitutional Information of
the 1780s, through the popular agitation of the nineties,
and the reviving movement in the 1810s.

**33.** p. 101, **Train up a child.** 'Train up a child in the
way he should go: and when he is old, he will not depart
from it' (Proverbs, xxii. 6). This biblical text features frequently in educational writings of the eighteenth and nineteenth centuries.

**34.** p. 102, **'New Institution'.** Owen delivered an
'Address to the Inhabitants of New Lanark...on Opening
the Institution for the Formation of Character, on the
1st of January, 1816'.

**35.** p. 103, **The child will be removed.** Owen's community plans always provided at least for the communal
education and feeding of children, though he occasionally
proposed removing them altogether from their parents' care
(or rather—as he saw it—lack of it). He was perhaps in this

attracted by the social orderliness of the Sparta of Lycurgus. See also note 46 below.

**36.** p. 104, **The area.** This was probably the first real children's playground. Other infant educators saw the importance of and provided such playgrounds. Wilderspin, for example, strongly urged their health benefits, and David Stow saw in these 'uncovered schoolrooms' opportunities for moral training.

**37.** p. 104, **The Sabbath.** For the fervour of the sabbatarian campaign from the late eighteenth century see Ford K. Brown, *Fathers of the Victorians: the Age of Wilberforce*, 1961. 'All violations of the Sabbath—newspapers, travel and the transacting of any business, but especially amusements such as cards, balls, assemblies or Sunday music, even walks in the country—seemed shockingly unchristian to the Evangelicals... The Sabbath was a Christian palladium; Christianity stood or fell as it was observed or neglected...' (pp. 15, 100).

**38.** p. 105, **Employed ten hours and three quarters.** 'Dale had worked the mills thirteen hours, with intervals of one and a half hours for meals. ...for some time during [Owen's] management the hours of work at the New Lanark Mills were fixed at fourteen a day (including two hours intervals for meals). It was not until January, 1816, that he was enabled to reduce the hours to twelve a day, with one and a quarter hours for meals...' (Podmore, *Robert Owen*, p. 92).

**39.** p. 111, **Knowledge of facts.** Owen's emphasis on facts and understanding is amplified in Robert Dale Owen's description of the teaching at the New Lanark schools (see pp. 153–61 above). To teach children relevantly was a precept common to Renaissance and Enlightenment educational thinkers, and in the work of the Continental reformers—notably Pestalozzi—the stress was on facts (or objects) and observation. Owen's theories and practice were, however, formulated before he had any contact with the Continental educationists.

**40.** p. 112, **Minds of children are yet unknown.** Owen

means 'unappreciated'. He is appealing for wider acceptance that children's potential is limitless, not for research into child psychology (although the place of New Lanark in the history of the empirical search for a greater understanding of children is a considerable one).

**41.** p. 113, **Evening lectures.** In fact a wide range of evening classes and entertainments was organised, including lectures on mechanics and chemistry.

**42.** p. 117, **Self-interest.** The vocabulary of Adam Smith and the classical economists. It was a central utilitarian principle that men seek pleasure and avoid pain. The general sum of happiness advances only because we individually address ourselves not to other people's humanity, 'but to their self-love, and never talk to them of our own necessities, but of their advantages'. Individuals cooperate harmoniously by saying to each other: 'Give me that which I want, and you shall have this which you want...' (Smith, *The Wealth of Nations*, 1904 edition, 1, p. 16). A society in which people are enabled to seek their pleasure and interest in this way is one which provides 'the greatest happiness of the greatest number'.

**43.** p. 119, **Drill exercise.** This amounted in practice to marching to the music of the fife. It was this and the dancing that more than anything else shocked the conscience of William Allen.

**44.** p. 126, **Greatest happiness.** See note 42 above.

**45.** p. 129, **Laws relative to the poor.** Owen, like Malthus and the Benthamites, who later framed the Poor Law Amendment Act of 1834, was opposing the system of relief dating back to the end of the sixteenth century, and sanctified in the Speenhamland system of supplementing wages (from 1795). It was in the nature of the remedy that Owen differed fundamentally from the Benthamites. Owen projected his community settlements in order to remove poverty by an act of collective social regeneration. The Benthamites sought to whittle away poor relief and deter from idleness.

**46.** p. 131, **Lycurgus.** Owen recalls in his *Life* that he read Seneca while at Stamford. It is sheer conjecture, but not unlikely, that he also at some time read Plutarch's *Life of Lycurgus.* 'Lycurgus the lawgiver' is credited with having remodelled the constitution of Sparta and made her from an anarchical into an efficient, disciplined State. Education was for him 'the greatest and most glorious work of a lawgiver', beginning at birth and even before (by the regulation of marriages). Discipline and health, for the sake of the state, were paramount. Owen, speaking in Birmingham on 5 October 1831, described the educational aims of the co-operators as being 'like what Lycurgus did with respect to war. He created the best warlike character; but we want to create one full of kindness' (*Co-operative Congress, Reports and Papers,* 1831–2, p. 17).

**47.** p. 133, **Whitbread.** Samuel Whitbread 'in the session of 1807...introduced into the House of Commons a Parochial Schools Bill, which was intended as part of a larger scheme of poor law reform...Mr. Whitbread was a member of the Whig Opposition and was conspicuous for his ability and influence in his party. The object of his bill was to enable overseers, with the consent of the vestry, to raise a sum for the support of education' (Adams, *History of the Elementary School Contest,* p. 65). The bill was rejected, among other reasons, because it might shake the foundations of religion and because books had been the cause of the French Revolution.

**48.** p. 137, **The Speech.** *Hansard,* VIII, 984, 1051.

**49.** p. 142, **New department of Government.** This was written a quarter of a century before the creation of the Committee of the Privy Council for Education. The resistance to government involvement in social organisation can be measured by the fact that of the 21,305 civilian officials employed by central departments in 1833, barely a hundred were employed by the Privy Council, Board of Trade, Home Office and the Mint taken together, as against nearly 16,000 by Customs and Excise (David Roberts,

*Victorian Origins of the British Welfare State*, 1960, pp. 14–16).

**50.** p. 142, **Seminaries.** One of the main virtues of Owen's educational activities was that they undermined the monitorial system. Owen relied on teachers and believed in the training of them. Brougham also, in moving for his Select Committee in 1816, urged a beginning to the training of schoolmasters, as he was to do again in the thirties. Although other forces were at work (including the activities of David Stow) to replace the monitorial system (and its perfunctory method of training teachers in monitorial techniques) by adequately educated and trained teachers, not until Kay-Shuttleworth's college at Battersea was opened in 1840 did the concept of teacher-training come into hesitant existence.

**51.** p. 145, **Malthus.** The famous *Essay on the Principle of Population, as it affects the Future Improvement of Society* by Thomas Robert Malthus first appeared in 1798. In it he asserted that 'the power of population is indefinitely greater than the power in the earth to produce subsistence for man. Population, when unchecked, increases in a geometrical ratio. Subsistence increases only in an arithmetical ratio...' (1966 facsimile edition, pp. 13–14). Unlike Malthus, Owen believed in the potential for expansion of agricultural and industrial resources. Owen argued from within his experience of the development of such resources, and actively promoted schemes which he believed would demonstrate the extent of productive potential.

## AN OUTLINE OF THE SYSTEM OF EDUCATION AT NEW LANARK

**52.** p. 149, **Robert Dale Owen.** Owen's eldest son, born in 1801. He played an active part at New Harmony, settled in America, became a well-known figure in the freethought and birth control movements, Senator, and finally (like his father) spiritualist.

53. p. 149, **Galleries.** This was a series of tiered steps at one end of the large schoolroom. Owen's arrangement at New Lanark represents a transition from the single-room monitorial school to the school divided into separate classrooms. Owen anticipated the galleries which were central features of Wilderspin's and Stow's infant schools, and which were used for teaching the whole school, or large numbers of children, simultaneously. For details and drawings see Charles Birchenough, *History of Elementary Education* (1938, 3rd edition), pp. 262–5.

54. p. 152, **Roman tunic.** The children were provided with this uniform, which has also been described as being of tartan material.

55. p. 153, **Miss Edgeworth.** Maria Edgeworth, daughter of Richard Lovell Edgeworth, with whom she wrote *Practical Education* (1798). She began writing children's stories in the 1790s, as an alternative to the adult fare to which children were normally subjected. 'It was Miss Edgeworth who really inaugurated for England the reign of didactic fiction. Though never losing sight of her aim, she also never lost sight of the amusement of her young readers...The chief charm of her tales...is that she not only wrote in the language of children, but, what is even rarer, from the child's point of view' (Helen Zimmern, *Maria Edgeworth*, 1883, pp. 41–2). It is understandable, given the books available, that Owen was adamantly opposed to their use in infant education.

56. p. 155, **Pestalozzi.** The influence of Pestalozzi on arrangements at New Lanark was a late one, and then probably restricted to this one area of the curriculum. For a discussion of Owen and the Continental reformers see Harold Silver, *The Concept of Popular Education*, 1965, pp. 148–56.

57. p. 159, **Miss Whitwell.** She was dismissed from employment by the company in the reorganisation of 1824. In 1826–7 she was in charge of the children at the Orbiston community.

## REPORT TO THE COUNTY OF LANARK

**58.** p. 166, **The source of all wealth.** Ricardo had published his *Principles of Political Economy* in 1817. The interpretation of his view that the exchange value of commodities was measured by the amount of labour which went into their production, and Owen's view expressed here, both contributed enormously to the growth of socialist economics in the twenties.

**59.** p. 169, **Communities in America.** Owen had in 1818 published an account of one of these: *A brief Sketch of the Religious Society of People called Shakers*, by W. S. Warder.

**60.** p. 178, **Derby Infirmary.** There is an account of these principles in Charles Sylvester, *The Philosophy of Domestic Economy as exemplified in the Mode of Warming, Drying and Cooking...adopted in the Derbyshire General Infirmary* (1819). This is an adaptation of a system in use from the early 1790s at the Strutts' factory at Belper, and consisted of warm-air heating—cheaper, more efficient and more pleasant than steam-heating. (I am grateful to Mr Graham Saville for this reference.)

**61.** p. 179, **Thick clothing.** Another principle Owen could easily have derived from Plutarch's description of Sparta in the *Life of Lycurgus*. Cf. also Locke, 'not too warm and straight clothing' (*Some Thoughts Concerning Education*, section 30). Also Rousseau's insistence on freedom of movement for children's limbs.

**62.** p. 179, **The Romans and the Highlanders.** The parallel was obviously important for Owen, even to the designing of the toga-cum-kilt for the children. See also note 54 above.

## THE ADDRESS OF ROBERT OWEN

**63.** p. 192, **False religions.** Owen had been driven increasingly since 1817 to define his position on religion. His vocabulary is at times atheist, at times deist, at times mystical, but his general position is always opposed to institutionalised, ritualised religion. Owenism from the late thirties became identified with secularism.

**64.** p. 195, **Rights of the sexes.** Anti-Owenites were particularly scandalised by his views on marriage (expressed in full in such publications as *The Marriage System of the New Moral World*, 1838). His protest against the marriage system which prevented divorce, yoked couples together where there was no affection, encouraged cruelty, and deprived women of any real rights, needs to stand alongside that of Mary Wollstonecraft, John Stuart Mill, Barbara Leigh Smith, and other campaigners for women's social rights. See also the extract from Owen's *Six Lectures*, pp. 208–10 above.

**65.** p. 196, **Labour note.** The labour note as a medium of exchange was in use at Owen's National Equitable Labour Exchange between 1832 and 1834. The note was intended to represent the value of an article in terms of the labour embodied in it. Since, in Owen's view, labour was the only source of wealth, the labour note was the true unit of exchange, which would replace an inadequate and unjust monetary system and lay the basis of genuine social cooperation.

**66.** p. 200, **Want of people.** See note 51 above. Owen's vision of human progress is here quite demonstrably different from that of the Malthusians.

**67.** p. 200, **A common pin.** The example of the growing division of labour used by Adam Smith in the first chapter of *The Wealth of Nations* ('One man draws out the wire; another straights it; a third cuts it; a fourth points it; a fifth grinds it...the important business of making a pin is, in this manner, divided into about eighteen distinct operations...', 1904 edition, p. 6).

**68.** p. 201, **Large cities.** Owen did not normally formulate such Cobbett-like attacks on urban society as such, although his community plans clearly imply a rejection of existing urban conditions. Cobbett wished to turn his back on industrial, urban society. Owen wished to re-organise it, to relate it to the needs of agriculture and of people. His schemes are firmly written into the history of nineteenth-century town-planning idealism.

**69.** p. 201, **Universities.** This is a rare reference. Another one occurs in his *Letters on Education* (1851): 'The Universities, Colleges, Academies, Schools, and all other Educational Establishments, must be gradually superseded. They are irrational and distorting moulds, and so worn out that they cannot be repaired. The population of the world must be gradually withdrawn from these, and placed and put within new moulds...' (p. 6). The new moulds, of course, are cooperative communities.

## [ONE OF] SIX LECTURES DELIVERED IN MANCHESTER

**70.** p. 205, **Divisions of human life.** Owen is concerned in many of his subsequent writings with this attempt at a rational division of society. In a Supplement to *Robert Owen's Millennial Gazette* (no. 10, 1 January 1857), for example, he divides the population of the world into twelve age groups.

# BIBLIOGRAPHICAL NOTE

There is a considerable literature of Owen and Owenism. The following is a guide to some of the most important landmarks, and to some of the themes discussed in the Introduction. Though not brought up to date, *A Bibliography of Robert Owen, the Socialist, 1771–1858* (second ed. 1925), published by the National Library of Wales, is the indispensable starting-point for any extensive work on Owen. The Goldsmiths' Library of the University of London has an outstandingly good collection of books by and relating to Owen, which can be approached through a catalogue, entitled *Robert Owen 1771–1858*, of an exhibition held in the Library of the University of London in 1958.

The fullest compilation of Owen's writings is his own *The Life of Robert Owen*, vols. I and IA (1857–8), with its invaluable reprints of Owen's reports, addresses, memorials and other documents in the period up to 1820. Max Beer's edition of the *Life* (1920) does not include any of these appendices. The Everyman edition of *A New View of Society and Other Writings* (ed. G. D. H. Cole, 1927, and subsequent reprints) is an accessible collection of some of the main writings.

Of the many books about Owen three are most valuable. Frank Podmore's *Robert Owen* (1906, reprinted 1923) is large, painstaking, and vital. G. D. H. Cole's *Robert Owen* (1925, 3rd edition 1965), is shorter and places Owen in his social and economic setting. Margaret Cole's *Robert Owen of New Lanark* (1953) is more interested in ideas, and makes use of some more recent research. A new biography of Owen is projected by J. F. C. Harrison; some initial material, seeking to relate Owen's views to those of Dugald Stewart and the Scottish Enlightenment, is contained in *The Journal of British Studies*, Connecticut, VI, 2 (May 1967). A centenary volume of Owenite studies is in preparation, edited by S. Pollard and J. Salt. There are chapters on Owen and the Owenites in W. A. C. Stewart and W. P. McCann, *The Educational Innovators 1750–1880* (1967).

On the industrial revolution, as a background to Owen's industrial career and attitudes to society, the two most useful general books are H. L. Beales' short *The Industrial Revolution 1750–1850* (1928, reprinted in 1958 with a new introductory essay), and the most recent economic history of the period, Phyllis Deane's *The First Industrial Revolution* (1965). For the social implications of industrialisation and the growth of towns, by far the most valuable book, though extremely long, is Edward Thompson's *The Making of the English Working Class* (1963).

For a discussion of literacy and the use of reading matter in early nineteenth-century England see Richard D. Altick, *The English Common Reader: a Social History of the Mass Reading Public 1800–1900* (1957). R. K. Webb's *The British Working Class Reader 1790–1848* (1955), which discusses a theme related to Altick's ('Literacy and Social Tension'), is useful in addition for its picture of the Society for the Diffusion of Useful Knowledge and utilitarian attitudes to social problems. The relevant sections of David Owen's *English Philanthropy 1660–1960* (1964) are the most recent and most valuable guide to the theme of charitable endeavour discussed here in the Introduction.

For a general background to the history of the ideas of the eighteenth-century Enlightenment the two most useful books are J. B. Bury's *The Idea of Progress: an Inquiry into its Origin and Growth* (1932, reprinted 1955) and Kingsley Martin's *French Liberal Thought in the Eighteenth Century* (1929, revised edition last reprinted in 1963). A more detailed study would make it necessary to look at Locke's *Some Thoughts Concerning Education* (first published in 1690); Helvétius' *De l'esprit* and *De l'homme* (suitable English editions of both appeared in 1810, the first translated by W. Hooper, the second by William Mudford; *De l'homme* contains the fuller statement of Helvétius' views on education); William Godwin, *Enquiry concerning Political Justice* (first edition, 1793, reprinted in a three-volume facsimile edition, edited by F. E. L. Priestley, 1946; vol. 1 is the important one). Ian Cumming's *Helvétius, His Life and Place in the History of Educational Thought* (1955) is extremely useful.

There is a brief and very bare account of the Manchester Literary and Philosophical Society (and of Dr Thomas Percival and the Rev. Thomas Barnes) by C. L. Barnes in W. H. Brindley (ed.), *The Soul of Manchester* (1929). An impression of Percival and his 'Enlightened' interests can be gained from a glance through the four volumes of *The Works, Literary, Moral, Philosophical, and Medical of Thomas Percival, M.D.... to which are prefixed Memoirs of his Life and Writings* (1807).

On monitorial education see D. Salmon, *The Practical Parts of Lancaster's Improvements and Bell's Experiment* (1932). On infant education see R. R. Rusk's sketchy but useful *History of Infant Education* (1933), which includes chapters on Owen and David Stow. Mary Sturt's *The Education of the People: a History of Primary Education in England and Wales in the Nineteenth Century* (1967), is a useful introduction to educational conditions, but unfortunately is better on the later part of the century. Other important general books (even if in need of revision in the light of modern research) are: Charles Birchenough, *History of Elementary Education in England and Wales from 1800 to the Present Day* (third edition 1938); J. W. Adamson, *English Education 1789–1902* (1930, reprinted 1964), which is good on the history of educational ideas; and F. Smith, *A History of English Elementary Education* (1931). The last one of these, together with the following, relates education most fully to other social movements: A. E. Dobbs, *Education and Social Movements, 1700–1850* (1919), and Brian Simon, *Studies in the History of Education 1780–1870* (1960), the latter an extremely useful guide to the whole educational and social picture of this period.

For a statement of Owenite views connected with the early cooperative movement see William Thompson, *An Inquiry into the Principles of the Distribution of Wealth most conducive to Human Happiness* (1824). For educational thinking in the Working Men's Association and Chartism see William Lovett, *The Life and Struggles of William Lovett in his Pursuit of Bread, Knowledge and Freedom* (1876) and his pamphlet written with John Collins, *Chartism; a New Organisation of the People* (1840). For a different aspect of the movement it is useful to look at John Saville, *Ernest Jones: Chartist* (1952).

For Owenite and other attempts at community-making, see the section on 'The Owenite Apocalypse' in W. H. G. Armytage, *Heavens Below* (1961). On New Harmony there is a short, modern survey in Mark Holloway, *Heavens on Earth* (1951, revised edition of 1966). An extremely interesting, though idiosyncratic, nineteenth-century account of New Harmony and of Owen himself can be found in John Humphrey Noyes, *History of American Socialisms* (1870, reprinted 1966). For a detailed, scholarly, and vivid account of New Harmony itself, see A. E. Bestor, *Backwoods Utopias* (1950), and for a closer account of education at New Harmony, the selection of correspondence edited by Bestor in *Education and Reform at New Harmony* (1948).

For all aspects of the labour movement in this period see G. D. H. Cole, *Socialist Thought: the Forerunners, 1789–1850* (1953). A short, but extremely helpful essay is H. L. Beales' *The Early English Socialists* (1933).

Finally, there is a discussion of some of the themes discussed in this Introduction in my own *The Concept of Popular Education: a Study of Ideas and Social Movements in the Early Nineteenth Century* (1965); this also looks at some related themes not discussed here, notably the late-eighteenth-century educational background, forms of resistance to educational provision, the Continental reformers, and educational ideas and movements parallel with those of Owen and Owenism.

# INDEX